THE FAMILY BUSINESS GURU

A SECRET GUIDE TO ALCHEMIZE CONFLICT INTO HARMONY, LEAD WITH CONFIDENCE, AND GENERATE PROFITS

AVADHI DHRUV

Difference Press

Washington DC, USA

Copyright © Avadhi Dhruv, 2024

All rights reserved. No part of this book may be reproduced in any form without permission in writing from the author. Reviewers may quote brief passages in reviews.

ISBN 978-1-68309-308-4

Published 2024

DISCLAIMERS

No part of this publication may be reproduced or transmitted in any form or by any means, mechanical or electronic, including photocopying or recording, or by any information storage and retrieval system, or transmitted by email without permission in writing from the author. Neither the author nor the publisher assumes any responsibility for errors, omissions, or contrary interpretations of the subject matter herein. Any perceived slight of any individual or organization is purely unintentional.

The information you obtain in this book is solely for informational purposes. It does not constitute nor is it meant to be legal, medical, financial, or other professional advice. The author does not make any warranties about the completeness, reliability, and accuracy of this information. Further, the scenarios presented may not be suitable for your particular situation. Any action you take upon the information provided is strictly at your own risk. You should consult with a licensed professional where appropriate. Neither the author nor the publisher will be liable for any losses and/or damages of any type in connection with this book.

The names and identifiers of the persons involved in the anecdotes presented have been changed for anonymity purposes. Any resemblance to any person, whether living or dead, is purely coincidental. Further, some anecdotes may be composites of other situations or experiences of the author.

Brand and product names are trademarks or registered trademarks of their respective owners.

Cover Design: Jennifer Stimson

Editing: Madeline Kosten

CONTENTS

1. Can You Earn Your Family's Love and Respect through Your Business?   1
2. True Story of Courage and Perseverance: Why You Can Have Your Cake and Eat It Too   11
3. The Path to Divine Harmony: How to Read the Rest of This Book   23
4. Creating Clarity in Mind for Your Goals   29
5. Business Partnerships with Family Members   43
6. Money, Negotiations, and Family Dynamics   53
7. A Spiritual and Systematic Approach to Delegation   73
8. Putting the Past in the Past   83
9. Finding and Owning Yourself in the Whirlwind of the Family Dynamics   93
10. Activate Attunement: The Divine Union of Masculine and Feminine Energies   101
11. Are You Ready for Unprecedented Business Success with Family Unity and Harmony?   109
12. Create Harmony in the World through Your Business Success and Family Values   121

Acknowledgments   133
About the Author   135
About Difference Press   137
Other Books by Difference Press   141
Gift for Readers   143
Other Books by Avadhi   145

Dear Dad – this one's for you!

I remember you always saying to people at social gatherings that you have two eyes – one eye being my mom as your queen wife and the other eye being me as your princess daughter. Then you would smile and say that – obviously – this makes you the king! I believe you are much more than that. <3

You are the reason I can dare to dream big. Knowing that I have you as my safety net inspires me to reach for the galaxies and beyond! You remind me to always stay grounded and live in gratitude no matter how high life may have me fly. Your heroic journey has been incredible. Your courage is unparalleled, your commitment is unshakable, and your heart is pure gold. You are the hero of our family and the king of the world to me!

"Entrepreneurship is not for the faint of heart. It requires tremendous sacrifice of your false self, so that your true self can shine. It demands the magnificence within you to show up fully."

— AVADHI DHRUV

1

CAN YOU EARN YOUR FAMILY'S LOVE AND RESPECT THROUGH YOUR BUSINESS?

Growing up with childhood insecurities and generational traumas can cause a lot of stress in one's family relationships. If your business is intertwined with family members, this can be a double-edged sword. It can feel like you can't handle the business when family relationships are tense, and at the same time, even if you feel like you want to quit the business, you can't really quit on your family. Family ties are quite strong; as they say, "blood is thicker than water," and family members often have many years and prior bonds of karma collected with each other; so much so that the souls incarnated in this lifetime can have difficulty clearing them as and when necessary.

THE KARMIC BONDS OF FAMILY

According to Eastern philosophy, souls take birth in this realm called the physical reality for the purpose of their own ascension. In this philosophy, it is widely known and believed that there is a theory of karma which I call "action-reaction," where for every action there is an equal and opposite reaction. Karma theory states that for every action, which includes a thought, feeling or emotion, word, and physical action, has a reciprocal energy that is bound to come back to the person who originated the action. In the case of family members, souls actually choose other souls as family members who they have past karmic bonds with – the karmic bonds that the souls are now ready to release and evolve out of for their own growth and evolution. If you look at the business dynamics with family members while having this understanding, the interactions can make a lot more sense.

If you had a traumatic childhood or emotionally unstable parenting or guardianship when you were growing up, you may have had experiences that caused you to feel insecure within yourself right from a very young age. This is exactly what had happened to Jack.

THE ROOTS OF INSECURITY AND GENERATIONAL TRAUMA: JACK AND MIKE'S STORY

When Jack was only two years old, he had a habit of biting and digging his teeth into anyone who picked him up without his liking. This was an innocent habit he had as a child for his protection. When people complained about his habit to his father, being stressed and enraged, his father, Mike, picked Jack up and threw him toward the window of their little home at the time. Of course, Mike didn't mean to cause a life-long trauma for his son by that action, but this incident created such a deep subconscious wound and trauma in Jack's mind that it caused Jack to believe that he was not good enough, that his father didn't love him or approve of him, and that he was basically a failure.

From that moment onward, Jack's mission in life became to do everything he could to please his father and make him proud. It was an unconscious decision, so Jack was not aware of it consciously, but all of his life decisions and business decisions later on in his life basically came from this deep-rooted childhood insecurity and the generational trauma that his father had passed on from the previous generations. Now, it was up to Jack to either heal it and stop the generational curse or keep passing it along down the line.

Mike was a very successful masculine man who had lost his father when he was just sixteen years old. After losing his father, Mike had to take on the responsibility of feeding and providing for his entire family, which included his mom, four sisters, and three brothers. Even though he was not the eldest of the brothers, Mike was one of the eldest and felt like the responsibility of the family was now on his shoulders and he must do whatever he needed to do to make ends meet and put food on the table. He couldn't go to college, as he had to finish his high school education and get started with a job right away. Ultimately, he was looking for a business that he could grow, and he turned into a serial entrepreneur out of sheer necessity. He later discovered this was also his innate drive and passion.

Mike started with a small shop that provided everyday supplies to his customers, including stationery. He opened the shop every morning, ran the store during the day, and closed it after cleaning up everything in the evening. As he learned how business worked through his initial endeavors like this store, Mike realized quickly that just one store would not be enough to feed all the mouths in his family.

Mike's father had left him some farmland in the village where he was born, but the farmland was taken away from his family pretty quickly due to some legal changes, so going back to farming was no longer an option for him. This started his journey into the ventures of serial entrepreneurship as he began to give any and all business ideas a shot, looking for the one that would truly be scalable and create enough income for his family as well as create long-term assets to leave a legacy for future generations, including Jack and his family.

THE FEAR OF FAILURE IN BUSINESS

The fear of failure in business can be overwhelming for any entrepreneur or business owner. It can stop him or her from taking risks in the direction of creating growth for their business. For a new entrepreneur, the fear of failure itself can stop them from taking the first steps. For someone with an existing business, the fear of failure can cause immense procrastination and stagnation. This is exactly what was happening with Jack. He felt unsure of himself and had lost his confidence, to the point where he felt like a total failure. He only wished that he could make his father proud. He felt like he was not good enough until his father approved of his decisions and actions in the business. The actual business results would show this, but alas, his mind was just not able to gather itself long enough to actually make a decision and then be able to stick with it.

THE FAMILY BUSINESS GURU   5

> *"Recognize that failures and struggles are stepping stones on the path to success."*
>
> — AVADHI DHRUV

The constant dilemma of which way to go and all the different options swimming around in Jack's mind caused lots of spinning wheels in his head but absolutely no progress in terms of actually moving the needle and taking actions that would move the business forward. He had been in business for all his life and involved with family members who had looked up to him maybe ten or twenty years ago, but now he felt like he had completely lost his family members' trust and respect. It was heartbreaking for him to hear his family, especially his father, almost yelling at him with disrespectful comments, scolding him and asking him to create business results that he did not know how he could create.

There were losses after losses happening in his business year over year. The last time the business made a profit was several years ago and now the cash flow was in a crunch. There seemed to be no way to go and no end in sight to Jack's constant misery. He thought about quitting the business and walking away from it many times. These thoughts of leaving came to him every single day. He wished he would wake up to a different reality, but it was almost like he was stuck in Groundhog Day and each day repeated the same pattern – family members calling, blaming, and complaining to Jack, asking for a better update than what Jack had to offer as far as the state of the business.

Issues with customers, employees, logistics, inventory, and cash flow all plagued Jack every day as he went to the office and tried to solve problems. He made payments to vendors that had overdue invoices, wondering where the next order was going to come from, having to decide what to do with outdated unsalable inventory items that would cause more losses if he got rid of them. He got irritated with his wife of twenty years when he came home because of all this stress from the office. Jack would bring the business home with him and think about the business all the time which affected his relationship with his wife and caused unnecessary arguments at home.

Jack's biggest fear was that he was a failure and would appear as a failure in his father's eyes. He wanted nothing more than to make his father proud. He also wanted to be looked up to and respected by his brothers, sisters, wife, daughter, and the rest of the extended family and community. He wanted to feel like he was able to provide for his family so the bills could be paid, and a house and food were available, so his family could live a good, safe, and secure life. All of this was at stake here and it seemed like everything was in jeopardy. *How do I escape feeling like a failure?* is the question Jack asked himself often. He also wondered about his legacy and what he could pass on to the next generations. *How will my future generations remember me?* These thoughts plagued him day and night and he could not figure out a way to turn this situation around.

> *"When fear of failure and uncertainty cloud your mind, remember that even the greatest successes are born from the ashes of setbacks and challenges."*
>
> — AVADHI DHRUV

CREATING HARMONY IN YOUR FAMILY BUSINESS

If you are reading this book, you may be well aware of the complicated dynamic a family business brings. Perhaps you have felt the agony and confusion that Jack felt, have lived with the fears of failure, loss, disappointment, and more, and are experiencing the uncertainty of the future that comes with these worries and stresses on a day-to-day basis. If this is your current reality, I'm here to tell you that it is possible for you to have harmony in your family relationships and create unlimited business success in a way that leaves you fulfilled, satisfied, and content. As difficult as it may seem to visualize this right now, it is my experience that allows me to say this to you. Through my own journey and the journeys of my family and clients, I can assure you that all of the challenges can be turned around. You can have the dream life with your family and for your business that you've always desired. Most of all, you can have the love and respect of your family that you truly wish to have. No matter how much debt, financial strain, or relational struggle your business currently may be in, or if you are thinking of starting something new in your business and you are afraid of losing family support, I can assure you that you can have the full support of your family while attaining the business success of your dreams and creating the legacy that you've always desired.

If you have been holding yourself back from seeing a different future for yourself, then I invite you to take my hand and come on this ride with me. I want to show you how your dream business and family life are possible, and everything you desire can come true for you, in just a few chapters ahead. You will feel the love, respect, and acknowledgment of your father or father figures, your loved ones, your friends, and your community members. In fact, those family members or friends may even come to you for advice on how they can shift their relationships, just by seeing you being the role model for a changed dynamic in your relationships and family business. You will be able to talk to your family members about any topic that may be coming up in your business regardless of any disagreements, differing opinions, or past-based judgments. Imagine having business meetings, phone conversations, or email exchanges with dignity and respect for your viewpoints and the viewpoints of your family members, no matter how much you are having trouble seeing eye to eye with them right now.

You will actually enjoy working with your family members, feel supported by them, and feel grounded by the fact that you have a wonderful team that you can rely on, which will forever be with you because they are your family. You may even have business relationships with your friends, and they may be like your family or they may be your business partners. In any case, you will also be able to create synergy within your friendships, which leads to productive conversations about strategy and future growth in your business.

When you feel calm and confident within yourself and safe in your conversations with your family members and friends, especially if they are your business partners as well, you will be able to make informed decisions from a place of clarity and focus in the direction of your business dreams. Making key business decisions is absolutely critical for your business growth and legacy creation. You will be very clear and decisive in your actions, and this will automatically make you a role model and leader that the rest of your staff will look up to, seeking your advice on things with a sense of respect and honor. When you feel respected, seen, and heard in this way, it will contribute to your sense of feeling accomplished and fulfilled, which is ultimately the feeling of being successful. Also, with this come the actual business results.

You will see a natural turn in your business: The losses and debt start to reduce as you make decisions that turn the negativity down and bring in more positivity in your thoughts and actions. This will increase revenue, improve the quality of customers who want to do business with you, and attract the kind of high-caliber employees who can help you create success in the long term. You will know how to engage the team members in your company to capitalize on their highest potential, and have them take care of your customers at the highest level so that your customers become raving fans of your business. These loyal customers will value your products and services, and want to do business with your company for years and decades to come. You will also have the clarity of a succession plan and legacy of your business long after you are either retired or have taken a step back from the day-to-day business operations. Either way, you will still know that the baby that you have nurtured for all of these years of your life is going to be taken care of and is in good hands. Knowing that your contribution to this business is continuing to make a difference in the world at large, and that it will last way beyond your lifetime, can be a great feeling and blessing to have.

Once you have healed your family relationships, created a complete turnaround in your business financially, and created clarity for the future succession of your business, your soul can rest peacefully. You can continue to live your dream lifestyle, go on exotic vacations if you wish, or just stay home and read a book when you feel like it, because all the other aspects of your family and business life are well taken care of.

As you are relieved from the day-to-day pressures of the business, you will have time and space to freely pursue any of your other interests, hobbies, societal projects, or passions, and contribute based on what you feel is your life's purpose and mission for the rest of your years. You will have the permission and the freedom to create the kind of impact you would like to have in the world through your own creations. This way, you will be living your life fully as your true self and creating a massive impact and a positive difference in the world. As your business grows in value naturally and automatically through the beautiful teamwork of your family, your employees, and your customers (raving fans), you will know that you have created and preserved generational wealth that your future generations will remember you for over the coming decades.

2

TRUE STORY OF COURAGE AND PERSEVERANCE: WHY YOU CAN HAVE YOUR CAKE AND EAT IT TOO

Growing up in India, I used to live in a joint family which means that my grandparents, my parents, my uncle, my aunt, my cousins and I lived in one big house together. I have very fond memories of my childhood living in India in the joint family style. I felt protected; my grandfather was a role model for me and the rest of the family, as he was a serial entrepreneur and had a rags-to-riches story that was immensely inspiring. He is, to this day, a recognized leader in our community. He built businesses and an entire global empire after losing his father when he was in high school. He gave shelter to all of his brothers and sisters, and took care of his mom, his wife, and his children. He is definitely a very healthy masculine man who has been the provider and protector of not only our family but also the entire extended community. People think of him with utmost respect, and today, at ninety years of age, he is still passionate about business and our family. Establishing strong generational harmony, unity, and legacy through the businesses he built has always been extremely important to him.

CHALLENGING CULTURAL GENDER ROLES

When I was born and as I grew up, I was the first child born in my generation, as my father is the eldest son to my grandfather. Traditionally, the families pass on business leadership from generation to generation, with the eldest male passing on the reins over to the eldest male of the next generation and then the oldest male of the following generation. Although I am a girl, as I was born as the eldest child to my father, who was the eldest child to his father, I have had this important duty that I always felt I needed to fulfill. I was always treated as a central most important member of the family, always provided for fully and protected very intimately, and at the same time encouraged to get educated, and possibly learn to take over the business from my father. Now being a girl, I also saw my mother, grandmother, and aunt as examples of the traditional female role; according to cultural norms, they got married and became part of their husband's family, lived with their husband, supported the household, raised the children, and basically did not get involved in the day to day of the business and did not work to bring in money and provide for the family.

My mom, and all of the females in the family, were provided for, protected, and mainly played the roles of nurturing the family, the home, social relationships, and the next generations, taking care of growing the family's legacy in that way. The gender roles were culturally decided, but this got confusing for me when I found myself being the only child to my parents and the eldest of the grandchildren in my generation.

As I grew up, I needed to decide what to major in for my college education. I had the example of my father who was a mechanical engineer by degree, and my mother, who was a pharmacist by education. Even though my mom was a pharmacist, she had never actually pursued pharmacy after finishing her education because she had decided pharmacy and the medical field weren't aligned with her values of holistic and natural health. She actually learned a lot of alternative therapies as ways to heal, and she loved caring for herself and our entire family through her unique holistic approaches. I knew I didn't want to go into the medical field for sure, so I decided to follow in my dad's footsteps and pursue an engineering degree. I've been good at systems and optimization, so Industrial and Systems Engineering appealed to me as a major, and that is the one I went with in college. After college, I gained important experience in the corporate world while working at large corporations like General Electric and Caterpillar Inc., through their leadership and technical development programs.

Shortly after working in the corporate world for a few years, I wanted to create freedom in my lifestyle and turned to my own entrepreneurial journey, so I could have my own business and not be an employee in the corporate world anymore. I decided to resign from my corporate job to become an entrepreneur. As I was learning my role as a new entrepreneur in my early years, I was very distant from the family business. My dad had been handling it for many years while I was in high school, college, and in my corporate job. I would talk to my parents once or twice a week and when I would talk to them, I started hearing from my mom about how stressed my dad had been recently. After speaking to my dad, he confirmed that he was stressed about the business situation.

NAVIGATING CHALLENGING FAMILY DYNAMICS

That theme went on until one day I decided to dig deeper and get to the bottom of what the stress in business was all about. My dad and I have always had a very open, honest, and loving relationship, and he shared with me that there were some decisions that my grandfather used to make in the business in prior years, which now my dad had to make. The differences in the opinions of the two generations – my grandfather's generation and my father's generation – were causing a lot of inaction in the business. My dad was frustrated and feeling demotivated about the state of the business because the growth was stunted, and this was affecting profitability.

I never thought that I would ever directly become a part of the family business. In fact, my father wanted me to stay away from the family business especially during the time when he was having stress and frustration within it, because he wanted to protect me from the stress as well. It was his love and protective instincts that wanted to keep me away from it all.

I was also afraid of stepping into the family business because, as a girl, I always felt like I didn't own any part of it, and that if I stepped in, I might step on my cousin brother's toes, which could affect our relationship. I've always had a close relationship with my cousin brother, and I deeply feared losing him if the business dynamics and money came into the picture within our personal relationship. I did not want to ruin the loving bond we'd shared for so many years, at any cost, and at the time, my money beliefs had me convinced that when money got involved, it just ruined relationships. I had to challenge and shift that belief and many other disempowering money beliefs in the following years.

So, I just kept staying on the sidelines and tried helping my father through other ventures, investments, and passive income ideas, so he could get relieved from the family business. I thought that if I helped create a new business that my dad could rely on, then he could get out of the family business, or maybe close it out, solving that problem for him. So having the entrepreneurial bug in myself, and being in my early years of the entrepreneurial journey where I was learning lots of different business models, and exploring and researching a lot of different new business venture options, I brought a few of those options to my dad as well and asked if he wanted to pursue any of those business ideas.

For a couple of years, he tried a few different business models and pursued some new business ideas; however, this was not solving the actual problems in the family business and I got a lot of calls from my grandfather who asked me to help my dad with the family business. I kept ignoring the messages from my grandfather due to my own doubts and resistance, until one day, I got a call from my uncle's son and he let me know how the family business needed immediate attention and full focus from all family members. That was eye-opening for me. I have always had a very close, sibling-like relationship with my uncle's son because we grew up together in the same home and the joint family. With me being the only child to my parents and with my uncle's son only two years younger than me, I basically always thought of him as my brother. When he told me that the family business needed attention, my focus had to turn toward the nitty-gritty of the family business itself. The more I looked into it, I found out that this was a much deeper rabbit hole I was now getting into!

My father always said that: "family business is a one-way street." You can only come in, but then once you're in, you can never go out. You're in it for life!

So, my father felt like he was trapped on this one-way street. "There's no exit plan in a family business," he always said.

One thing that I noticed which was bothering my father was the succession of the business. He felt demotivated because he was worried about who would take over the business after him, if I didn't. If there's no one to take it over, why should he spend his energy and all this hard work to grow it further? He felt lost in all of this and the current dynamics and differences in opinions with his business partners, which were his father and brother.

As I became more aware of what was bothering my father, I decided to get involved with the business just long enough to where we could turn it around and position it to be saleable. I still was not sure about taking over the family business completely, so I wanted to create an exit plan and thought that if we could sell it at a capital gains profit, then my parents could use the proceeds in their post business retirement years and I would stay away from it for the rest of my years. My father always wondered about retirement, and my mom said she was already retired! We decided that my dad would retire into the business rather than out of the business, for now. That was a new concept to him!

> *"Scarcity comes from living in the fear of losing. Abundance comes from living in the possibility of creating. Choose to focus on possibility and create your own experience of abundance!"*
>
> — AVADHI DHRUV

STEPPING UP IN THE FAMILY BUSINESS

When I got more involved in the nitty-gritty of the business, we started looking at the financial statements and I started asking questions. I now realized a lot more of what was really going on. Some of what I discovered, I couldn't even believe!

As I asked questions and investigated what was going on, my dad revealed all of the things that were plaguing him. I found out that the business he had built had become dependent on a couple of the vendors who were supposed to be serving the business and its growth but were instead just taking advantage of what the business had to offer. These vendors were not contributing to its growth. Also, on top of that, the people who my dad had trusted to keep the business running were in turn disrespecting my dad and calling their own shots, which were not always in the business' best interest. I decided that I needed to step into this and figure out what was really going on. I wanted to bring back the happiness and the smile on my dad's face. So, the little girl in me stepped up as a young adult who was ready to take on the challenge in order to see her dad happy again. This whole situation was also impacting my mom, and I later learned it was also affecting my entire family. Little did I know that this one gesture from my heart would lead me to become the chief transformation officer of the global brand that is my family's business empire.

I also got deeper into this when I went to India to help plan my brother's destination wedding. I was so excited when my brother finally found the woman that he wanted to marry, and they got engaged! Weddings are a big deal in India, and they're made into a huge celebration so we can all make lots of family memories together. As I had played a major role in planning my own destination wedding a couple years prior, I was excited to help plan my brother's destination wedding as well. As I got to India, where I would be for a few months, I started asking everyone questions, expecting everyone to be excited about planning the wedding. I quickly realized that the excitement I was expecting was totally missing. Everyone seemed to be extremely busy with day-to-day life and one crisis or another.

As I dug deeper, I found out that a lot of the crisis was connected to the business, and I didn't know why everyone was so focused on the business when there was a family wedding to plan! I got into the business stuff further just to find out what was stopping everyone from being excited about the wedding planning. I had opened Pandora's box, and I couldn't believe what I found out! I was shocked at what was going on in the business dynamics within the family. It affected all of the relationships and of course affected the business itself to the point where the stress of the family relationships permeated into every aspect of business. The stress from the business had caused strain in relationships within the family on a very, *very* deep level.

The elder sister in me, being very protective of my brother, stepped up and organized a meeting in the boardroom of our company office. I interviewed every single person in our family individually, and then collected all the information and various perspectives into a single cohesive picture in order to prepare for the board meeting beforehand. I created a strong, positive intention for the meeting, wrote our culture's core values on the white board of the boardroom, and then welcomed all family members on the day of the meeting. My mom kicked off the meeting with a story of a flock of pigeons who were all trapped in a hunter's net. While none of the pigeons could get freed up on their own, if they all flew together they could get to a place where the net could be chewed out by some mice and then they could all be freed up through the unified effort. The moral of this story became the theme of our board meeting that day. This was a unique time when all the members of the family and leadership team came together and shared their ideas, which I wrote on the white board to capture everyone's thoughts and we came up with productive solutions.

That meeting was a huge turning point in the trajectory of the business empire! Immediately I was asked to organize another meeting to follow up on this first one. I did a lot of energy healing work for all the souls involved, before and after each meeting that followed, and through the collective intentions of all the loving bonds of our family and my utmost efforts in bridging any and all communication gaps in the process, a massive amount of karmic burden seemed to have been relieved and the business was on its way toward a harmonious future ahead.

This was just one layer of many more layers that were yet to be peeled off in this massive family dynamic that I had ended up getting involved with.

Over the next several weeks, months, and years ahead, we brought harmony in communications, we created unity in decision-making, we bridged gaps in understanding, we created a stronger brand presence for the group of businesses globally, and we set healthy boundaries and structures in place for the benefit of all, while releasing karmic patterns and sabotaging beliefs from our fields.

Today, as the chief transformation officer at Prabhat, I create and facilitate the long-term growth strategy for the family business along with our team's annual goals and quarterly rocks. I lead the team so we can all be aligned in our actions toward a unified direction by creating systems, processes, and effective business policies. Like captaining a ship, or even a fleet of ships, to reach a predetermined destination, my role includes everything from managing compliance items like insurance renewals to developing a marketing strategy with the team, from creating metrics to track to aligning our sales efforts with that to facilitate sustainable growth with stability and strength. Through my role, I nurture the company culture by inspiring the right hiring and team empowerment decisions. My role also allows me to bring in the spiritual principles and tools for individual and collective growth of our team members through personal development and heart-centered alignment. Bringing a holistic approach to business, we expand our awareness, consciousness, and comfort zone at the subconscious level of mind, and create unprecedented levels of harmony and business results for the entire brand and group of companies. We win as a team and operate with unity. We create our customers into our raving fans and celebrate all the growth and success while having fun along the journey together!

> *"All your dreams are possible, when you choose to step outside your comfort zone."*
>
> — AVADHI DHRUV

3

THE PATH TO DIVINE HARMONY: HOW TO READ THE REST OF THIS BOOK

If you are ready to finally feel relief in navigating the complexities of running a family business, the following chapters in this book lay out the path that is designed to take you from where you are to the ultimate bliss of Divine Harmony. I call it – The Path to Divine Harmony. As I always say: "Harmony has money in it!" As you embark on this journey ahead, you will naturally find yourself attracting and keeping more money in your life, within your family, and through your beloved business!

THE PATH TO DIVINE HARMONY

In this process, first, you will understand that you need to determine clear goals for yourself to focus on and the goals need to be based on your own desires, not other people's expectations.

Then, you will know the ins and outs of business and family relationship dynamics so you can overcome any pitfalls from masculine and feminine energy imbalances that are causing resentment, fear, and disrespect among family members, leading to micromanagement and procrastination in the business. You will also prepare for the next steps of cultivating and implementing the abundance mindset by creating synergy and win-win-win solutions for all people involved.

Next, you will be introduced to the concept of healthy boundaries, what they are and why they can be helpful for you, and then learn how you can start setting clear boundaries in your role in the business. As a result, you will make new space for achieving your goals with the help of your relationships by switching conflicts into cooperation and alignment.

Thereafter, you will understand fully that the business and family harmony you desire is not a solo task, it actually requires the magic of a team effort, so you will become clear on the importance of effective delegation, right hiring and training processes for team members, and how continuing to maintain healthy boundaries can help with running your business effectively.

Then, you will understand how to uncover and release any subconscious blocks that may be limiting you, realize the patterns and habits not serving you, and strengthen yourself emotionally while putting the past in the past.

After that, you will understand why it is important for you to know yourself and your values rather than trying to overcompensate for other people's demands, how to own your sense of worth, individuality, self-expression, and confidence, and why this is key for both your business success and family harmony.

You will clearly understand how you can step into your Divine Self, embody your true essence, and become in tune with your higher self by making God your ultimate partner in business and family life.

Further, you will identify all the fears that can stop you from achieving your dreams even after creating your strategic harmonization plan.

Finally, you will understand the entire path, how a life of success and harmony is possible, what the steps are, and how you can realize your dream of business success and family harmony!

The Path to Divine Harmony is about creating unity, trust, respect, and a loving environment for all. It is ultimately rooted in compassion. Sometimes it can look like having or facilitating a healthy dialogue. At other times it can look like setting a clear boundary in terms of a process, a policy, or a consistent way of doing things that creates results. When Divine Harmony comes into the picture, it is important to understand that it includes and needs to include the divine masculine and the divine feminine energies. The union of the masculine and feminine energies, also understood as the left-brained and the right-brained approaches, is what brings harmony in all situations. The Path to Divine Harmony then can basically be achieved by balancing the energies and creating a whole-brained state in business and life.

LOVE WINS OVER ALL WARS

Know that love is the greatest power above all. Leading with love and staying in love is the key to winning, for yourself and for your family, for generations to come. Love can bring people together. Love can also heal wounds. Only love is real. It just looks different in various situations and at different points in time. When you come from love, your soul is at peace. You know in your heart what the truth is, and you feel truly fulfilled. That is the true test of whether you're coming from love or not in any particular moment. Love is a choice you can make from moment to moment. It is a powerful choice and requires courage in day-to-day life and business decisions. Knowing when to speak and knowing when to hold your tongue is a delicate dance that you can master by consistently staying in and coming from love. Being rooted in compassion is key to mastering the art of being and operating from love. Looking out for one another, thinking about the long-term vision, intentions, benefits, health, and win-win for your team, your customers, your family, the community, and the world, are natural byproducts of being rooted in compassion and living from love in your everyday life. The Path to Divine Harmony is about walking with love being present in your heart and being rooted in the foundation of compassion, for yourself just as much as for others.

> *"Love is always uplifting, honoring, empowering, and motivating toward yourself and others."*
>
> — AVADHI DHRUV

It is not an easy path, but it is worth every ounce of energy and awareness you put into it. Being true to this path will pay dividends to you for the rest of your eternity and the eternity of your family and all the generations to come. Are you ready to embark on this journey and take the steps forward to creating this brand-new reality in your life and business? If yes, I'm ready to take you through the steps and guide you as you enter into the unknown with me holding my hand. Let's explore a whole new world for your family business together.

> *"At the end of it all, it is the person you become through the process of reaching toward your goals that is your most important reward."*
>
> — AVADHI DHRUV

4

CREATING CLARITY IN MIND FOR YOUR GOALS

Decision fatigue is a big deterrent to success in business.

Gerard struggled with making decisions in business and constantly felt like he wasn't sure which way to go – to do this or to do that. Since a young age, he had always been told what to do and had depended on his father who made all the major decisions in his family, so he had been protected from taking risks when it came to making big decisions in life and business. Later on, when Gerard didn't have anyone to tell him what decision he should make, and when nobody dictated the decisions to him, he got confused about the direction ahead and felt extremely lonely and vulnerable. The loneliness he felt was a sign that he didn't have a way to tap into the most powerful source from within when it came to steering the direction of his life and creating progress in his business. If you are feeling like Gerard, there are a few different points you need to be aware of and understand.

OVERCOMING DECISION FATIGUE

Firstly, decision-making comes with its inherent risks. It is risky to make decisions, because once you decide on something, you are stepping into the unknown and will need to face the consequences of your decisions, whatever they may be.

Another thing to understand is that every decision, in life and in business, has its benefits and consequences. These can be thought of as pros and cons. The benefits are the pros that usually attract you toward making that particular decision and the consequences are the cons that usually stop you and deter you from it. If you are unable to accept that every choice you make comes with both these sides of the coin, the pros and the cons, then you're going to have a very tough time making a decision and creating progress. However, once you understand this simple fact, you can become a master at making decisions, no matter how big and scary they may seem to you in the beginning.

So, for example, let's say that you need to decide what to have for dinner today. The two options are Italian or Thai. If you choose Italian, the pros are that the restaurant is close by, and the food will be mildly spicy, if that's your taste. The con is that you'll have to eat alone, as let's just say that your friends don't want to eat Italian today. If you choose Thai, the pros are that you will have the company of your friends because let's say that they want to eat really spicy food today, and the food will be really spicy, if that's your taste. The con will be that the restaurant will be further away for you all to get to. Now, you can see how both options have their pros and cons. Just understanding and acknowledging that there are pros and cons to both, and accepting these facts can give you a huge boost in your decision-making abilities. This is because when you resist the cons of each option, it keeps you from benefiting from the pros of that option as well, and you keep oscillating between the two options like a ping pong ball. In this case, you can't decide if you want to go to the closer restaurant and eat by yourself or go to the one further and eat in the company of your friends! When you can accept that there is magic in accepting all the facts, you can get beyond the ping-pong effect and truly evaluate the options wisely.

So now, let's take a business example. You need to decide whether to hire a new team member, an assistant, to help you take some of the tasks off your plate. So, the options are to hire or not hire. If you hire an assistant, onboard and train him or her well, the pro is that you will have freed up your time to do other high-value tasks in your business. The con is that you now have an additional responsibility to manage, lead, and provide for this new team member. If you don't hire the assistant, the pro is that you have more flexibility and less managerial responsibility, and the con is that you now have to do all the tasks yourself so this could slow down and limit your growth activities for the business.

Having clarity about your big-picture priorities and your long-term vision, key intentions, and goals broken down into quarterly rocks, is going to be key for this next step. The clearer you are on your values and your overall direction in your life and business, the easier it'll be for you to make your decisions on a daily, weekly, and monthly basis.

You will need to weigh the pros and cons and see which option's pros outweigh their cons.

So, imagine a scale in your mind ⚖, and evaluate each one of the options at a time. Put the pros of the first option on one side of the scale and the cons of that option on the other side to see which side turns out to be heavier. If the side with pros weighs more than the side with cons, this indicates that the first option may be a good option for you to choose! Next, take the second option and weigh the pros and cons of that option on the scale in a similar way. If the pros outweigh the cons for this second option, then this indicates that the second one may be a good option for you to choose. Once you evaluate all of the options available to you by weighing their pros and cons on the scale, you can choose whichever option's pros most outweigh its cons.

Finally, tapping into your intuition is the best and most aligned way to ultimately receive guidance in the process of making your decisions. When you tap into divine guidance, which you have access to 24/7/365 and which is available to you at no additional cost, you will make the most headway in confidently making decisions in your business! For tapping into and having your intuition guide you, you need to develop a relationship with it so you can build trust. There is a very special process that I guide my clients through for developing this level of trust with their intuition which requires practical application and interactions beyond the scope of this book. If you want to learn how to tap into your intuition, which is your innate genius – the part of you that has all the answers for you so you never have to feel lonely in your business and life again – email my team at team@avadhi.guru for a special price on my private coaching packages.

UNDERSTANDING INTENTIONS VS. GOALS

During one of my private client sessions, a question came up, "What is the difference between an intention and a goal?" It was very interesting what followed after that.

Are you feeling lost in the sea of unfulfilled intentions and unachieved goals, unsure of how to reach your dreams? Do you find yourself confused about how to set the right intentions and goals, and what the difference really is?

If so, you're not alone. Many individuals struggle with understanding these concepts and how they can work together for you so you can realize your desires. Below, we will delve into the distinctions between intentions and goals, and explore how they complement each other in the manifestation process.

Goals originate from masculine energy, and are designed for bringing focus on specific, measurable, actionable, realistic, and time-bound objectives. Goals must be grounded in the physical realm and require a tangible action-oriented approach.

On the other hand, intentions emanate from feminine energy, and are driven by desires, creativity, and imagination. They are expansive, limitless, and can be unrealistic from a logical standpoint. Intentions need to be most aligned with the feeling of having the desired outcome and do not need to be specifically action-oriented in a tangible way.

Goals provide a clear sense of direction and require action steps to take. They guide individuals toward tangible achievements and provide a roadmap for progress.

Intentions are rooted in possibility and trust. They

invite individuals to surrender to the Universe and allow inspired actions to unfold naturally. Intentions are more about being in alignment with desired experiences rather than taking specific actions.

The purpose of setting intentions is to expand one's being and align with the vibrational frequency of desired experiences. Intentions serve as heart-centered desires that transcend logic and tap into the infinite possibilities of the Universe.

Goals provide a sense of direction and accomplishment, guiding individuals toward tangible outcomes. They offer clarity and structure, allowing individuals to track their progress and take actionable steps toward manifestation.

Intentions focus on the feeling of the desired outcome, and setting specific goals aligned with those intentions can facilitate co-creation. These goals serve as action-oriented steps that support the manifestation of intentions.

It's essential to remain detached from the outcome of specific goals while staying connected to the overarching intention. Trusting the Universe and allowing for alternative outcomes to unfold can lead to unexpected manifestations beyond your initial expectations.

As an example, an intention of mine could be manifesting the publication and success of my second book, driven by the desire to make a positive impact on readers' lives.

Within this intention, a specific goal could be to create a detailed book proposal by a set deadline. This goal provides actionable steps toward the overarching intention while maintaining a realistic and measurable approach.

Understanding the distinction between intentions and goals is crucial for manifesting business success. By harnessing the power of both masculine and feminine energies, individuals can co-create their desired reality. Remember to stay connected to the feeling of your intentions while taking inspired actions toward your goals. With trust, faith, and alignment, you can manifest miracles and true success in your life.

RECOGNIZING THE TRUE CHALLENGE

When I was hired on as a project manager for a specific project about researching new options for warehousing and distribution services, and for managing the transition of inventory from the current warehousing contractor to a new one, I started off by doing a lot of research and finding options which could work, as I thought this was the exact project I needed to complete.

When I got to the implementation phase of the project, I noticed that there was more to the story than met the eye. Actually, there were a lot of other factors of the business which needed to be addressed and this required a full upgrade in all areas of the business' operations. I also recognized that there was a fear-mongering and bullying situation at hand. The current contract with the warehousing company that this particular business had was controlling everything in their business, so the owner didn't have full authority. The vendors of this business were underperforming and overcharging for their services.

This was causing issues in the family business, between the business partners, and led to indecision and constant fear of loss in the owner's mind. Once I could see this picture very clearly, I realized that the project of switching warehouses was not the main thing that needed to be done. I started to look at the full picture and we opened up the entire contract that this business had with their contractors, which included warehousing services and also other services like bookkeeping and accounting, HR management, marketing and sales, customer service, legal recommendations, etc.

TAKING CONTROL OF THE BUSINESS' FINANCES

I recognized that the biggest obstacle in the way was that the business' bank accounts were controlled through a contractor where the family business did not directly have ownership over its own bank accounts. As soon as I learned this, I decided to speak with the owner and see if he could bring in another family member who could be trusted to help with the migration of the business' bank accounts. The owner was able to bring a close family member in to take full control and independent responsibility over the company's bookkeeping and accounting system. Separate bank accounts were created and the owner took full financial control over the company's cash flow. We also set up the company's bookkeeping and accounting through a new software, and the company hired an independent staff accountant to do the company's bookkeeping going forward. This way, they first took full control of the company's finances. This in itself was a huge project and once completed successfully was a huge win.

Next, we started taking control over the other areas of the business in the order of priorities; the next one was sales and employee management. We hired a high-level executive to fully take charge over sales and customer relations while also managing the current sales team, and this was another bold move that helped the owner get full control over the company's revenue stream. We had already started to look at all of the company's expenses, fixed and variable, and trim down any expenses that were destructive or excessive and non-productive, so that the cash flow could start to turn around. The owner was able to take the management of cash flow in their family's hands and got full control over it.

In this way, the company's contract was updated and the costs of services were reduced by over fifty percent. Further, due to energetic shifts and a lot of new clarity that was created in the minds of the entire team, the family business' relationship with their contractor was renewed and harmonized during this process, where they continued to do business together for a long time thereafter. The owner now had a completely independent team for his business' operations including bookkeeping, accounting, sales, marketing, customer service, order processing, HR, legal, and tax filings. We also took control of the company's data by taking all of the company's paperwork virtual and creating an entirely remote team that could access everything through cloud-based software and systems. They started to have all their company and customer meetings occur over video calls and did not need physical office space or constant travel anymore. That also cut down on the costs of the company significantly which boosted the company's cash flow.

TRANSFORMING COMPANY CULTURE

As all of the projects I did with the family business started to unfold and come together, the entire company structure changed. Not only did we transform the structure of the company, but in this process, we also transformed numerous limiting beliefs and fear-based thoughts into empowering beliefs and courageous worthiness-based feelings, emotions, and actions. Everyone on the team at the family business was transformed from the inside out through many more projects that were done over the years, and this was the biggest reward for everyone in the end.

> *"Confidence is not a function of knowing EVERYTHING outside of you. Confidence is a function of knowing who YOU are within yourself!"*
>
> — AVADHI DHRUV

After these initial layers of transformation, I could see that there was a challenge to keep all the team members who were now working remotely on the same page and aligned with the company's culture. I noticed that the company didn't currently have a congruent culture, and so not having clarity on the company's brand was causing a big challenge. I spoke with the owner and we decided that we needed to work with a brand strategist and get crystal clear on the company's brand and unique values, and have all of this documented in a clear brand guide that then could create consistency and clarity for all team members, current and future. The company's website also needed to be updated and was having technical issues, so we took on a brand strategy project, and had a brand sourcebook created for the company, documenting the company's vision, mission, and core values along with all the other unique aspects of the company in a very in-depth manner. Then we also documented the visuals for the brand, and used the company's brand values and the visuals to have the company's website updated in order to create consistency in all of our messaging for the market-facing materials going forward. Identifying the company's vision statement, mission statement, and core values was a complete game changer. I encourage you to also come up with your company's vision statement, mission statement, and core values if you don't already have those clearly defined. This is your company's brand foundation, and having clarity on this piece is critical for you as a business owner.

When I shared this story with my father, he said that my title was not a project manager in this case, that it ought to be the CTO, i.e., chief transformation officer, as mentioned before.

Originally, the owner of the family business who had hired me thought that the warehousing project needed to be done because his father had asked him to have that done. As it turns out, it was not really a goal the owner wanted to achieve for himself. What was most important to the owner was to turn his business around and have peace of mind for his family's future. As we worked through the various projects, the owner ended up getting what he really wanted. He felt freed up and happy in the new reality of his business! The moral of the story here is that the goal you may be currently focused on could be based on other people's opinions, or it may be a more surface level issue, but not based on what you actually want and what your business actually needs. It is important for you to introspect into what you really want, and then look at all the areas in your business that need to be addressed, so that we can tackle the root of all the problems, not just the surface level symptoms. This is the way that your business can truly flourish.

SETTING CLEAR GOALS

When you are dependent on other people's opinions, judgments, or expectations for determining your goals in business, you can often be like a puppet with the strings being pulled by the puppeteer, feeling a sense of hopelessness and being controlled. You've not been fully aware that the goals that you are running after may not even be what you actually want for yourself. You may have just assumed that these are the right things to go after. What if you let go of what other people's opinions are, set their expectations aside, and from a clean slate, explore what your own objectives are, what would actually work best for you, and create your goals for this year accordingly? This could be a game-changer for you. Perhaps you have not done this level of independent goal-setting before, in which case you may find this exercise quite foreign because it's new. However, you will learn that it's quite freeing because now you are only seeking answers from within yourself and nowhere outside of yourself. If you had no one to please, what would you want your goals for your business to be for the next twelve months? Ponder this question and write what comes to you. Taking on goal-setting in this way for your business is key to developing strength of character for yourself as a leader in your business.

> "It is NOT your job to make other people's dreams come true. It is your duty to create the life of YOUR dreams and then live it fully, so that other people can have permission to do the same in their lives! This is how you serve the world. This is how you live your purpose. This is how you fulfill your DESTINY!"
>
> — AVADHI DHRUV

In this chapter, you have learned about how to combat decision fatigue. You have also learned the crucial distinctions between intentions and goals, understanding how they operate in tandem to manifest desires. By exploring the transformative journey of taking control of a business' finances and culture, you've discovered the power of setting clear, internally-driven goals to unlock true growth and fulfillment in both your business and personal endeavors.

5

BUSINESS PARTNERSHIPS WITH FAMILY MEMBERS

Robert was extra frustrated today. I could see it in the frown on his forehead, when he said, "I had a call with my father today and it did not go well." His father was angry again and wanted him to obey his command as far as the business decisions were concerned, and Robert did not agree with him, but he could not say anything back to his father. Out of respect, he thought that he should keep his mouth shut. So, he did.

I asked him, "If you are keeping your mouth shut and keeping your opinions to yourself regarding the business decisions because you respect your father, then why is there a frown on your face!?"

He was puzzled, and as if for the first time in the day, he realized that he actually had a frown on his forehead and there was tension showing through his face. He tried to wipe off the frown with his hand rubbing at his forehead as if his fingers were going to be enough to get rid of the tension, and he said, "Oh no, no, that's nothing. It's just that I've been a bit frustrated."

I asked him, "So what is the cause of your frustration?"

He said, "It's just that I am not able to explain to my father that his perspective of making this particular business decision does not work in the current reality. We're making a lot of losses because we're carrying excessive inventory and taking risks when we deal with outdated inventory and unsaleable products over time. He thinks that making more production increases profit through economies of scale, when actually that way of thinking is not serving the business – it is harming the bottom line! I heard him out completely," and he paused. The frown on his face got lighter as he got his words out and he felt heard and seen in that moment.

"So why can you not tell your father exactly what you just told me?" I asked. In response, he said that his father would probably get angry, because he had a different opinion, and he thought that his opinion was the only right one.

I said, "And what would happen if he gets angry?"

Robert got very uncomfortable and said, "I don't like conflict. If I say something and it is not received well, then that would create a very uncomfortable situation for me. I'm uncomfortable with conflict, so I would rather avoid it and not go there."

Now, this is where the conversation turned into a coaching session. "Would you like to know how to hold your stance in a conflict situation?" I asked. "If you're going to create a well-functioning business and a harmonious relationship with your father, who is also your business partner, you're going to need to develop these skills of holding your own position in a conflict situation and speaking your truth anyway." As soon as he heard this,

Robert was intrigued. He had not imagined that it could be possible to hold his stance in a conflict situation and speak his truth anyway. When he heard me say that this was a possibility, he was all ears.

FOUNDATIONS OF TRUST AND RESPECT

First and foremost, we will need to understand that the foundation of any relationship is based on trust and respect. Now, in family dynamics, it's important to realize that often, because we already know or think we know a lot about each other, we tend to filter whatever the other person is saying through a lens of, "I already know what he or she is going to say," and therefore we barely listen to what someone is saying or attempting to say.

For example, when Robert's father started to say something to him, Robert already thought he knew where his father was going to go, and when he thought he already knew what was coming, his mind shut itself off and went into its own internal chatter instead. Robert started thinking that his father was going to say the same thing again, ask the same thing he asked yesterday, and there would be conflict if he said anything opposite to what he already knew his father wanted. He felt that there was no point in stating his truth, or listening to his father, and basically Robert started getting frustrated internally but could not express his feelings outwardly. As a result, he buried his anger within, which turned into resentment over time.

Now when I talked to Robert, I said, "If you think nothing can change with your father's thinking, then that leaves you trapped in the same space that you are in now, and nothing new can happen. If you would like something new to happen, then we need to first create the space for a new possibility."

Robert was open and listening with curiosity. I said, "Next time you speak with your father or when he calls you, start with a clean mental state. Release what he will say that you already know, and everything that has happened in the past, and just for this one time, practice listening to what he actually says. With the words that he utters, pretend that they are new and different from the words you have ever heard before. There is no need to speak much or to think about what you're going to say back to him next, but instead just practice being present, and listening to what he's saying with generosity. Do this experiment once and then let me know how this goes."

Robert said, "Okay, I'll do it." The next day, he came back with amazement at what had happened! Robert said that he had a call with his father, and this time he was present, and he listened to every word that his father uttered, without getting distracted with his own automatic thoughts. Robert said that he felt so loved at the end of this call with his father! Robert was surprised because he hadn't said a word to his father, he especially hadn't uttered what was on his mind earlier about his differing opinion, but also that his father had not said anything different than what he had been saying in the prior phone calls they had had.

How is it possible that Robert's feelings and experience of his call with his father had shifted from one of frustration, anger, and resentment to one of complete acceptance and love? I said to him, "The power came from your generous listening, being open to a new possibility, and the shift in perspective. When you listen to a person from a clean slate, you unconsciously give the other person permission to come from a clean slate toward you as well. When you listen to someone with generosity and presence, you can actually hear the truth of their intention behind their words much more clearly and especially when these are family members and loved ones involved, the intention is always one of love, care, and concern. When you stop assuming the worst in your mind, and start listening for the best in the other person's intention for you, what you are doing is shifting your perspective internally, and the external circumstance changes accordingly. That is why it is often said that, change your perspective, and you will change your world!"

> *"Love is the language of the Divine, while attachment is the false image of love when there is a disconnection from the Divine."*
>
> — AVADHI DHRUV

A POWERFUL EXERCISE TO TRANSFORM YOUR RELATIONSHIPS

To put this concept further into practice, I challenged Robert and asked him to do the following exercise: "Write 100 things about your father that you truly love and admire." I said. "A hundred things?!" He asked. "Yes, at least a hundred," I answered. He took his notebook and started writing the list, and while the first few points took him a bit of time, once he got into the flow of it, he didn't even realize when he had made it all the way to 120 things and he had surpassed the 100 things I had asked him to write! Most importantly, he now felt completely different about his father after doing this exercise. He told me that he felt much more connected with his father and there was a sense of safety created in his mind regarding their relationship. "Great work!" I said, "and now, choose another person in your business who you have a tense relationship with, and do the same exercise. Write 100 things that you truly love and admire about that person." Now, Robert agreed wholeheartedly, and went on to write a list for his other business partner in his notebook. He felt completely rejuvenated after doing this exercise for the second time! This way, he was able to shift his perspective on the various people around him, and this completely transformed his relationships and interactions with them.

If you are ready to change your dynamics with your family and within your business, do this simple exercise which Robert did. Write 100 things that you truly love and admire about that person who you have a tense relationship with. Notice the difference after you complete the exercise, and share it with your loved ones or send me an email at team@avadhi.guru and let me know how you feel.

NAVIGATING MASCULINE AND FEMININE ENERGIES

Healthy masculine energy is all about providing and protecting. Healthy feminine energy is all about being present in the moment, receiving, being in the flow, and staying connected to intuition. When wounded, masculine energy can get aggressive and defensive. When two people both in their masculine energy try to talk things through, this can lead to conflict as both are in the action mode and problem-solving mode, but they are not in the receiving mode.

If this happens, it is best to recognize what is happening, let things settle down a bit, and shift yourself into your feminine energy state. Get present, be receptive to the other person's words as well as their emotions, and allow them to fully express their opinions without contradicting them for what they are trying to say. If the situation calls for it, let the other person provide a solution, and allow their healthy masculine energy to show up in this process. When the overall dynamics return to a good balance between masculine and feminine energies, this will help create harmony and peace between you and the other person involved.

STAND IN YOUR TRUTH WITHOUT DISRESPECTING OTHERS

Let me give you an example of how to stand in your truth without disrespecting others.

John was making some demands of his coworker, Ally, which she didn't feel comfortable with. Ally used to comply with John's demands to avoid disappointing him, fearing it would strain their relationship if she disagreed. However, this dynamic led to negative impacts on her health, well-being, and self-esteem – and then it impacted the business finances. So this time, Ally didn't want to go that same route. Now she wanted to stand in her truth and voice her opinion about what worked for her, but she was afraid and didn't want to disrespect John in the process.

Oftentimes, fear of not being good enough, fear of being misunderstood, fear of losing a relationship, fear of abandonment, etc., can be playing under the guise of "wanting to be respectful." This is what was happening with Ally.

The key to understand here is that true respect is never rooted in fear. Being respectful has nothing to do with avoiding conflict or holding back because of fear. In fact, let me explain what respect actually is.

Every soul is born in this physical realm with their own free will. This is an inherent birthright. Therefore, fundamentally being respectful to someone actually has to do with respecting their free will. Whether you agree with the person or not, and whether you understand where they're coming from or not, you can still choose to respect their free will. This looks like acknowledging that they have free will in this life and accepting that they can do or not do anything that they wish. No one else can control them, and wanting to change someone else is in itself disrespecting their free will.

So, if respect is not rooted in fear and the need to control someone, then what is it actually rooted in? Well, respect is rooted in deep compassion.

Now that you understand what respect actually is, you should also recognize that you have your free will, and you also need to honor that from within yourself. You need to be rooted in compassion for yourself first and then let that compassion overflow toward others. When you stop making yourself wrong for your needs, you can then honor others and that's how you stand in your truth without disrespecting others!

So back to the example, now we know that both John and Ally have free will. Respecting John means respecting his choices and decisions. Ally trying to control or change him would be disrespectful to his free will.

Similarly, Ally needs to respect herself by honoring her own free will and her needs as well.

So, to address this situation, Ally first recognized that she needs to let go of the resentment or need to change John from within herself. Once she was able to fully accept John for who he was and how he was being, without any judgments, she now had the power to speak her truth as well. She also needed to let go of her fears and judgments around her own needs. As soon as she gave herself permission to honor her free will, she felt safe to express herself calmly to John.

As Ally was not making John wrong for his behavior, John also opened up and heard her concerns when she shared them with him. By expressing their truths honestly and compassionately, Ally and John could have a productive conversation. They were able to find common ground through respectful dialogue and compassion, and create a win-win solution fostering personal growth and an even more harmonious relationship.

Just as Ally and John were able to resolve the issue by respecting each other's free will and by being compassionate, you can also apply these principles to ultimately find win-win solutions in your business and family relationships.

> *"Respect isn't rooted in fear, it's rooted in admiration and gratitude toward one another."*
>
> — AVADHI DHRUV

In this chapter, you have learned the importance of building trust and respect in business partnerships, particularly when family members are involved. By navigating the dynamics of masculine and feminine energies and understanding how to stand in your truth without disrespecting others, you've gained valuable insights into fostering harmonious relationships and achieving win-win solutions in your business.

6

MONEY, NEGOTIATIONS, AND FAMILY DYNAMICS

When money, negotiations, and family get involved together, the dynamics become very interesting, to say the least. If you are in the midst of strained relationships because of the complexities of negotiations with family members, this chapter is where we will unravel all of that and more. Understanding the concepts described in this chapter will help you create healthy boundaries which are key to achieving the harmonious growth and success you desire in your family business.

Let's start with the very basics first.

Here is a very important distinction that I want you to understand – the difference between love and attachment.

THE DIFFERENCE BETWEEN LOVE AND ATTACHMENT

This may be a widely misunderstood and misinterpreted

topic in our world today. It is critical to understand it and then implement changes accordingly.

Love is the unconditional power of trust and confidence that emanates from the heart. Attachment is a byproduct of an insecure mind, a mind that is filled with unworthiness and fear of one's own existence.

Love is the state of consciousness which arises from deep compassion and the connection with one's self and the entire cosmos! Attachment is a desperate longing of such deep connection, yet actually just a futile effort to fill the void and the disconnection with one's self and the world with external tangible validation like things, people, positions, etc.

Love is always uplifting, honoring, empowering, and motivating toward one's self and others to allow all beings to become better versions of themselves. Attachment weighs heavy on us and people around us. It becomes limiting and restrictive, counter-productive, and ultimately is just an effort to give oneself a false sense of significance.

Love is freeing, generously allowing self-expression, while attachment is binding, suffocating, restrictive, and controlling toward true expression.

Love says: "May the Divine power that created us, shower all the heavenly blessings over my offspring."

Attachment says: "I must be the one to give all the worldly pleasures and things to my offspring."

Love says: "May I be proud of my children and many generations ahead."

Attachment says: "I want my children and people around to be proud of me."

Love is the true and authentic language of the Divine, while attachment is the false mirage of love which shows up when there is a deep disconnection from the Divine.

MONEY AS ENERGY

Money is just a form of energy because everything is energy at its core essence. Money is also a man-made concept that represents an exchange of value. However, money means different things to different people. What is money for you? Have you ever really thought about this? We all grow up with basic, fundamental beliefs about money, which come from the collective consciousness, your family's history and family line consciousness, the place where you were born and brought up in, the culture you came from, and even the religion that you were exposed to in childhood.

Money beliefs also come from your parents and role models as a young child, and the other people around you when you are in your early childhood. After that, they come from your own experiences in life and what you personally chose to believe to be true for you and in the world. Have you taken stock of what money really means for you? What is money according to your definition? It is very interesting to do this exercise, because when I asked this one simple question to all of the team members in my client's company, every single person had a different answer to the question, "What is money?"

Someone said money is "freedom, abundance, and very valuable" while someone else said money is a "big problem, it is scarce and hard to get, and it's a lot of work to get it and keep it." Yet another person said that money is a "resource – and an important resource at that – and very helpful to have and use." Another person said that money was "the bane of our existence and the source of all of the struggle in the family." This person believed that if they only had enough money to go around for everyone, then only the family relationships could be saved.

Are any of these answers right or wrong? Not really! The fact is that these answers are individual perspectives coming from different people with different beliefs and observations. Each of these answers is just the person's own take on money, not what money is in itself. Money is also the currency in our economy which is made to be circulated, and it needs to stay in flow to actually create value and abundance in the world. So, you may realize here that there is money as the truth of what it is, and then there is money as the perspective that you see it with – which is actually your money story, your story about money. Whether money brings you freedom or it brings on problems is dependent on your money story. Whether money serves you or is hard to get is basically part of what you believe to be true in your money story. Money at its root is just neutral; it is just a form of energy that is here to take form and return back to its energetic form once its role is complete.

One thing I know about money as energy is that it loves having a purpose, just like everything else in this loving, friendly Universe does. It loves to stay in flow, freedom, and circulation; it loves to be appreciated. Money only comes to those who appreciate it, value it, and love having it. This is why understanding your comfort zone around money is very, very important.

Your comfort zone around money can be understood in two stages, the first one being your comfort zone around being able to bring in and attract money to you in your energetic field, and the second being your ability to save and invest it to grow it for the long term. So, what is your money blueprint? What is your energetic comfort zone for bringing in money right now? And what is your money comfort zone for being able to keep and grow the money where it can have babies and even grandbabies if you'll allow it to?

> *"Experiencing abundance and fulfillment in life is a direct result of being true to one's SELF within."*
>
> — AVADHI DHRUV

UNVEILING YOUR MONEY BLUEPRINT

Often, I see that people in the same family unit usually share the same money blueprint but may have slightly different perspectives or stories about it based on their specific experiences during their upbringing. So, you may notice that subconsciously you are programmed to think of money and behave around it in the same way that perhaps your parents were, or grandparents were. You may not even be aware of all of the beliefs you have around money, but you probably can notice a trend in your family. Perhaps your family always has a lot of money coming in but could not hold on to the money, so the money left as soon as it came in. Perhaps your family has a history of not too much money coming in but then being able to hold on to the money that does come in. Perhaps your family even holds it too tightly and perhaps even hoards it sometimes. Perhaps your family has a history of being able to bring in more money consistently and being able to keep the money and invest it to grow it consistently in the long term. Or perhaps your family has a completely different history than the examples above.

The truth is that childhood trauma and feelings of insecurity are actually scarcity in disguise. Creating harmony in your business family and life begins with recognizing this fact. Creating and preserving generational wealth is not possible by staying in scarcity, it is a result that can only be achieved through Divine Harmony.

In any case, the money that has a pattern for coming in and staying, or not, is the programming that is probably built into your subconscious. Perhaps you are able to create and manifest money, and it comes in, but then you notice that somehow it goes out as fast as it came in. If this is the case, there could be a scarcity paradigm running the show not only in your subconscious mind but also in your family unit and the entire family consciousness. In this case, the healing needs to happen not only within your individual subconscious mind but also in the collective of the family unit. In fact, you may have been called to do the healing work for your family unit by first being the example of that healing within yourself and then contributing to the change in the collective consciousness of your family so that consciously or unconsciously other people in your family have permission to move into their healing process as well.

While everyone has free will and they could choose whenever it's the right time for them to participate in the healing journey, you taking part in your own healing journey might be a catalyst that can accelerate the readiness and willingness of your family. This occurs because energetically, you are very closely connected to the rest of the people in your family, whether you feel relationally connected at the moment or not. So, here's what I want you to do: consider that you taking a step toward your healing journey in regards to your finances and your money story is you actually taking a stand for a brighter, more positive financial future for your entire family unit, your ancestry, your future generations, as well as the collective of humanity. This is a big step to take, and I congratulate you for being willing to take that step.

Since family units are foundational to a functioning community, and well-functioning communities are foundational to a wealthy and thriving world, it is in the favor of humanity that you take this journey for yourself and start to heal yourself fully in your finances and relationship with money.

BEGIN YOUR HEALING JOURNEY

This healing journey begins with you intimately examining your current beliefs around money. These beliefs can fall into two major categories. The first category is one of scarcity, lack, hardship, struggle, burn out, and unworthiness. The second category can be one of abundance, freedom, choices and options, enjoyment, pleasure, and ultimate truth of worthiness and self-respect. Now, take a notebook or a journal and a pen and write on the top of the page: What are my current money beliefs?

With that journal prompt, let all of your thoughts that come up when you think of money flow through your mind while you just jot them all down. Do not try to analyze, rationalize, explain, or justify any of the thoughts that come to your mind. Just let your thoughts flow, and capture everything as is that comes through in your journal so that we can take a cold, hard, authentic look at it. Once you have finished writing down everything that came to your mind, without rereading it, flip to a new page in your notebook and write this new question: What would I like to feel about money and believe about money in my life ahead?

Then, start writing everything that flows through you – every idea or thought that comes up in this category. Let every thought flow and jot everything down without judging it, without trying to justify anything, and without trying to fix anything. Once you have noted everything that comes up in this category, now you can stop writing and go into the next step, which is reflection. Self-reflection is the key to recognizing the truth about the current state and then choosing the new state of being.

Now go back to the thoughts you jotted down in the first category and note how many of those thoughts are empowering for you, and how many of them are disempowering. Count the numbers of disempowering and empowering thoughts in that category and put the number down in your journal. For example, if you've written twenty thoughts and you notice that fifteen of them were disempowering and five of them were empowering to you, then you would just have "disempowering – fifteen," and "empowering – five," on your journal notebook page.

Now, go to the pages where you wrote down what you would like to feel and what you would like to believe about money and read what you wrote there. Notice how many of those thoughts were empowering and how many were disempowering and then jot down the number of empowering thoughts and number of disempowering thoughts from this section as well.

Once you have the numbers of empowering and

disempowering thoughts on both pages, you will be able to see what's really been driving your financial life and reality up to this point and it will also give you a direction of which way to proceed in order to create your new financial reality so that it can serve you in your life. Take all of the disempowering beliefs and thoughts that you identified and question them – are these really true? Are these absolutely the truth? If not, then what is actually true? Once you ask yourself these questions, you'll get the answers and then you can wisely choose which beliefs you would like to keep in your mind for your future ahead.

SETTING BOUNDARIES TO CREATE THE SPACE FOR HEALTHY NEGOTIATIONS

Boundaries are a very important concept to understand. When you think of boundaries, you may think of separation. The truth is that there is no separation in the ultimate unified field of consciousness, only in the three-dimensional physical reality that we have incarnated in. According to Eastern philosophy, we have all taken on identities and roles that are limited to this particular lifetime, and this includes the family relationships and dynamics. So when it comes to any family relationships that are involved in your particular business situation, it is important to realize the truths of the ultimate reality as well as the physical reality, and the fact that these truths exist simultaneously. When you can hold these truths as true for you at all times, your interactions with family or in your business can start to be seen differently.

When you speak to another person, whether it's a team member or family member, keep in mind that they are just another soul playing their particular role in this lifetime, as actors play characters in a movie. At their heart, that person is energetically part of the same universal consciousness as you are; therefore, there is no separation between you and them. At the same time, that person is here to play a particular role as their character, and you are here to play your role as your character in the proverbial movie. While they are in their character's role, they have free will to speak and act as their character would do in a particular situation. You, while you are in your character's role, also have free will to speak and act as your character would do in that particular scenario. Looking at the situations and people with this understanding, you can stay completely neutral and in loving acceptance of them while playing your role as well. Through your free will, you can let them play their character out completely from their free will as well! This becomes key in any internal negotiations with family members in business. By having faith and trusting the Universe to guide the process, you can come up with creative and sustainable solutions for all.

FOUR TYPES OF NEGOTIATION OUTCOMES

Further, here is the model of the four types of outcomes from any negotiations.

- **Win-lose**: When Party A in the negotiation wins at the expense of Party B, so Party B loses.
- **Lose-win**: When Party A gives in due to fear, and Party B wins as a result of it.

- **Lose-lose**: When both parties end up losing, often because of quarrels or misunderstandings that cause lack of communication, and both parties are unable to come to a creative solution due to lack of trust.
- **Win-win:** When both parties each get what's most important to them and win in the long term.

Even though it seems like there are four different types of outcomes in this model, the win-lose and the lose-win types are both just lose-lose eventually, because when one party wins at the expense of the other party, they both end up losing in the long run anyway. Therefore, it all boils down to just two types of outcomes at the end of the day. Either everyone loses, which is often what happens when you operate from scarcity, or everyone wins, which is guaranteed to happen when you operate from abundance!

So, always keep these four types of outcomes in mind during any negotiations you are part of in your business. Negotiations, when they are unhealthy, can feel like emotional blackmail, fear-mongering, and threats. If you notice any of this happening in your business, this alone can be killing your business, and you must address this as soon as possible. Negotiations, when they are healthy, often look like productive conversations involving a factual review of a situation and then creative problem-solving with all parties together in an effort to create a win-win for the long term. Healthy negotiations are necessary for any business to function in a productive manner. Avoiding negotiations is a big reason for a business to fail, so taking on negotiations and turning them into a healthy dialogue is key to business success.

THE ULTIMATE NEGOTIATION PROCESS

Things get tricky especially when there are family members involved due to the emotions that can create entanglement in these conversations. This is where healthy boundaries are key to creating the right space for the conversation. For example, it can be helpful to create different channels of communication for different purposes. It may be beneficial to choose an email chain as a channel for a particular business negotiation. Especially if it is with family members, keeping records of the conversations in writing, and not engaging in any verbal discussions or phone conversations for that particular negotiation can be helpful. Verbal discussions and phone conversations are best reserved for more casual family related topics, and keeping the business and personal interactions separate via different communication channels is a key technique that I've used in my life and with my clients to create highly successful results.

When there are multiple topics of negotiation, it's usually best to choose one topic at a time and straighten that one out before moving to the next topic, rather than pursuing too many topics at once and not landing any sort of clarity on any of the topics as a result. Just like when a complex knot needs to be unraveled, one must pull on one of the threads in the knot at a time. Once that first thread is loosened, the knot automatically loosens up and becomes easier to undo. Then we can pick another thread to loosen and untie from the knot, and this way, one by one, the various threads get unraveled and the entire knot, however complex and tight it may have been at the start, can now be fully undone and resolved! If you had tried to pull on too many threads of the tight knot at the same time, this not only would have made undoing the knot extremely difficult, but any one of the threads could have also made another thread tighter, further entangling the knot and making it even more complicated than it was to begin with.

It works the same way when you are dealing with family relationships intertwined in a business. Since emotions are always involved when it comes to relationships, especially with family members, knowing which thread to pull on first to untie the knot is extremely important. The way to know which thread to choose is to first find the thread that has the least amount of emotion attached to it. When there is less emotion involved, the facts can be looked at much more clearly and the thread can be untied pretty smoothly. Once that thread is untied, a new level of trust that is built from that process can now help you untie the next thread which may have a higher level of emotion attached to it, and then once again, you must find the thread with the next least amount of emotion attached to it and focus on that thread next. In this way, you can quite systematically untie a highly complex knot no matter how deep the emotions run in your business and family situation.

After navigating through numerous types of negotiations in business within my own family and for my clients, I have created the following step-by-step process that can be applied to any negotiation, especially for the negotiations that are involved in a family business. Understanding and implementing these steps in the stated order as follows can help you create an ideal outcome in any situation!

Here are the steps in the Ultimate Negotiation Process:

- Step 1: Have all involved team members write at least five things which are great about this negotiation situation.
- Step 2: Notice any conflict and downgrade the conflict into a disagreement by detaching from your own opinion and stop making the other company's opinion wrong.
- Step 3: Get really clear on what your facts and non-negotiables are.
- Step 4: Based on the information the other party is providing, get clear on what seems to be their non-negotiables.
- Step 5: Keeping all of that in mind, create a counteroffer to send them.
- Step 6: Communicate the pieces of accountability – if they have promised things that are not being met, use that in the counteroffer communication back to them.
- Step 7: Continue the negotiation process until you achieve an agreement that is a win-win for all!

SECURE YOUR FAMILY'S FUTURE

A lot of entrepreneurs and business owners are frustrated, especially in their initial years in business, because they keep making losses and can't even get to breaking even. They have to keep putting money into the business, month after month, and that seems to be the only way to keep the business alive. This takes a toll on the entire family of the business owner, and it can definitely affect your family's future and your legacy. It literally feels like you are throwing away money repeatedly, getting burned out, and eventually you'll just have to quit. This is a very common phenomenon, and most young entrepreneurs are new to this situation, so it's really important to understand that this type of situation can happen.

If you are tired of making losses in your business and want to know how to turn it around to finally break even, and start making profits, this section is for you.

The very first step is to decide. This may sound strange, but I'm serious when I say this. *You* have to start by making a firm, non-negotiable decision that you're turning your business around this year. There is enormous power in your decision, and if you have been allowing your business to operate at a loss, without having a strategic plan, it is most likely because you have not made a firm decision. You may have been wishy-washy with your intentions; you may have been fussing around; or even stressing around hoping that the more you "worry" about it and harder you work, the more likely it is to turn around, but sadly, that's not how it works. In fact, worrying about it and stressing or working harder is not the solution and that path will only burn you out faster.

So, cut that out, stop the hustle, and pause long enough to take a deep breath and decide. When you decide, you literally cut off any other options there may have been, and you clearly choose your direction. You set this as a clear goal and make it the top priority for you this year. You also radiate the faith and trust in the higher power that the achievement of this goal is indeed possible, in this particular timeframe you've set!

I was working with a client who had a business that had been operating with losses for the past twelve years! The company kept borrowing money to keep the business afloat, in the hopes that the next year would be better, but the same pattern continued. When I stepped into the role with this company, the first thing we did was to create clear goals and one of the main goals we created was to make at least one dollar of profit that year. A single dollar of profit meant that the company was at more than break even. That's all. Now, we not only created this as a main goal, but we actually also decided as a team that this was going to be a reality for the business within that year.

Now, once you have decided, then you can align all your actions and next decisions based on the direction you have clearly identified. After this, we started to look at every single expense on the company's profit and loss statement, and evaluate the need for it.

At this point, it would serve you to understand that not all expenses are created equal. Below are the four categories of expenses:

- **Destructive expenses**: These are expenses that are actually damaging your business and these expenses should be *eliminated* as soon as possible from your business (e.g. extra fees, customer complaints, etc.)!
- **Protective expenses**: These are expenses that are necessary and provide peace of mind for you in your business. These expenses should be in place and be *minimized* based on

your business' needs (e.g., insurance, legal entity, legal agreements, etc.).
- **Maintenance expenses**: These are the basic operational expenses. These expenses should be *maintained* on a healthy balance for business to operate smoothly (e.g., salary/wages, office space, utilities, etc.).
- **Productive expenses**: These are required for long-term business growth. These expenses must be *proactively increased* because they are an *investment* into the business, which brings in an ROI for the company's long-term future (e.g. personal growth, marketing, sales, brand strategy, continuous improvement of systems and processes, networking, coaching, mentorship, mastermind, etc.).

So, once you have eliminated the destructive expenses, minimized the protective expenses, and managed the maintenance expenses, you need to start looking for ways to *increase* your productive expenses. This is the *key* to not only turn your business around, but also to create a healthy and profitable business for the long term. Oftentimes, you must even increase your productive expenses while you're addressing the other three categories, but regardless, you must know the difference and make the most of every dollar you invest into your productive expenses. You also need to put your time and energy into productive expenses in order to get the best results.

Additionally, you need to look at the products that you are selling and the cost of those goods / services. If you are charging less than the cost of the product or service, you must raise your price to be above the cost or reduce the cost to be below the price, *or* you will have to just stop selling that product or service. This requires a little bit of simple math, but it is a must for you to calculate!

Now, lastly, you must maintain faith that all the life lessons that are meant to come to you through your business *are* going to come up as a part of the process. So, there's no point trying to escape the lessons. Embrace them, take rest when you need it, and then keep moving forward. At this stage, it is really important to get the help you need to achieve your goals. Depending on how important this is to your business, you may need to find the right resource and a mentor who can guide you through the process and that way you can ensure that you achieve your goal and ideally, dare I say, also enjoy the process! Life is too short for you to be miserable through the journey.

So, in summary, make a decision that this year will be the year you turn your business around and set this as the single most important goal for you, then get the guidance and create accountability for you to stick with that goal until completion. Take actions to clean up your business expenses and set the right pricing, and then engage your family members' strengths to create a powerful team effect which should create a new sense of security in your mind and a level of synergy in your family that can translate into your business success. Remember that maintaining faith along with having harmonious relationships is at the core of a profitable business!

"More time does not equal more value. Higher quality results equal more value. Always be results oriented & seek to provide greater value from your work. That's the way to create abundance and fulfillment!"

— AVADHI DHRUV

In this chapter, you have learned that money is not just a currency but a form of energy, and it can be influenced by individual perspectives shaped by upbringing, culture, and personal experiences. Understanding your money blueprint, creating healthy boundaries, negotiating from a place of abundance, and managing your company finances responsibly are all vital steps toward building a prosperous business and securing your family's future.

7

A SPIRITUAL AND SYSTEMATIC APPROACH TO DELEGATION

In this chapter, you will understand fully that the business and family harmony you desire is not a solo task, it actually requires the magic of a team's effort, so you will become clear on the importance of effective delegation, right hiring and training processes for team members, and how continuing to maintain healthy boundaries can help with running your business effectively.

When I started my coaching and consulting business while still managing the family business, I quickly got overwhelmed, burned out, and learned that there just weren't enough hours in a day for me to do everything myself without starting to lose my health, my relationships, and my sanity. I knew, either I'd have to give up my passion business or withdraw completely from the family business.

I didn't know how to make this decision! I tried to figure out which one to keep and which to quit, and kept bouncing back and forth between the two, one day thinking of going one way, and the other day thinking of going the other way. I couldn't come to a clear conclusion.

Neither of those were options I realistically could choose. My soul wouldn't let me give up on my passion business and my family needed me in the family business.

So, in that moment, I knew that I'd definitely need to have a team to rely on for all this to work and create synergies between the two businesses for both the ventures to be successful.

One day, I was at an appointment where I met a lady who was talking about how she raised her kids. Being the only child to my parents, I'd always heard how much time and attention it takes to raise just one child. So, I had assumed that it would take double that amount of time and attention to raise two children! In certain respects that may be true, however, what I learned from the lady was quite surprising to me! She mentioned that raising two children (or more) can actually be easier than just raising one in many ways. Basically, the gist of what she said was that when you raise one child, the second one watches the first and learns a lot of things automatically. So the first child in effect raises the second one, and if there's a third one, the same thing happens, and so on. So, as long as you inculcate the ideal values in the first child, that can help raise the second and third and so on. This was an inspiring idea to me!

I thought of how this could also work in terms of the businesses. I always referred to my passion business as my baby anyway, so I thought of the family business as a grown-up child and the passion business as a younger child and how they can both learn from each other and grow together! Instead of me trying to raise two different children separately, I could allow them to watch each other and learn from each other. This released a lot of pressure from my mind, and also benefited the businesses because when one business did trials and errors for certain aspects, establishing a system and a set of processes that worked, the other business could learn from that automatically. This would save a lot of time and money for the second business; it did not have to learn everything the hard way! I started to look for the lessons from one business and apply them into the other one and this became a new pattern that contributed to enormous growth and a consistent winning formula for success on both sides without burnout on my end and that of my team.

BUILD A BUSINESS THAT RUNS WITHOUT YOU

Imagine that your business is like a sandcastle. Wind can easily blow it away or the water from the waves of the ocean can easily wash it away. In this case, you have to constantly be around your castle to protect it.

Now, with some pixie dust and the wave of a magic wand, imagine that your business has turned from the sandcastle into a magic castle that is built with durable material so the wind can't blow it away and the water can't wash it away.

Next, imagine that there are all these little people inside your magic castle operating different functions and there is all this activity that keeps the castle strong, well-maintained, and serving its purpose.

Now, you have the freedom to step away as you like or engage with the people inside the castle as you see fit, so you can truly enjoy the magic that the castle creates in the world and be in awe of what you have built.

Is that something you would like to have for yourself? Let me tell you how to turn the sandcastle into the magic castle then!

First, you need to get crystal clear on who you are as a brand, what your values are, what your company's mission and vision are, who you serve, what principles you stand for, and what you are not for. All of these elements clearly and cleanly define your brand. My company packages this as a document called the brand guide. This document becomes a highly valuable brand asset that will serve to guide your company and team for generations to come.

Next, you need to balance your masculine energy with your feminine energy. You need to understand that running a company yourself requires you to be in your masculine energy while hiring a team to run the business for you requires you to be in your feminine energy. Being in your feminine energy is about being open to receive support. It's about staying in gratitude, and loving and nurturing your team as well as yourself. It involves being true to your brand and values so that you can be an inspiration and a motivational leader that your team can look up to. Always remember that your business is a reflection of you. Your team is a reflection of you. You, as the leader, will have influence over how your team behaves. So, be intentional with the culture you create and then live into it.

> *"Wealthy people have a team, not because they are wealthy. Wealthy people are wealthy because they have a team! The wealth principle of giving and receiving is at play here – riches come to those who are willing to share their resources with others and are open to receiving assistance in their journey."*
>
> — AVADHI DHRUV

Finally, create systems and procedures to guide your team in day-to-day operations and decision-making. Creating clear policies for guiding decision-making is going to be key for you to be able to build your business in a way that it wins and runs without you!

A SYSTEMATIC APPROACH TO DELEGATION

Your zone of genius is made up of a set of talents and skills that sets you apart, makes your work product uniquely valuable, and gets you the best return on the effort you put in. This is the kind of work you are naturally designed to be doing, and you may even be gifted in it! Get as zoned in on your zone of genius as possible and eliminate, automate, or delegate the rest. The more time and energy you spend in your zone of genius, the better off you will be and the more your business will generate cash as a return. Let the other tasks be done by other people whose zone of genius that task is. Doing this will increase productivity multifold and also raise the overall vibration you and your team are living in!

If there are any family members involved in your business and if there are any strained relationships in the business, that can add to the stress in business and cause delays in making business decisions. Recognizing that every person has their unique strengths and then harnessing those can create true team effort, emotional stability, and family harmony, fostering clarity for empowering key decision making.

A client I was coaching had certain family members who were not helping with decision making and certain strengths were being wasted. For example, my client's wife wasn't as involved, and his kids weren't as well. He had actually kept the family away from the business because he wanted to protect them from the business stress and strain, but the fact was that they were feeling the stress anyway. Your family feels the stress you're going through because they are so closely connected, so it was actually helpful for the wife and kids when they were brought in as team members who could now help and do something to move toward their goals for the year.

When engaged well, family members can be the most loyal and dedicated team members you can ever have! We brought all those strengths together for this client and that created a lot of peace of mind for the business owner. He was able to feel secure, not only about the business, but also about the legacy of his family, because now he knew his family would know what to do with the business even without him. This family will be able to benefit from the business and take care of it for generations to come!

> *"When you're an individual, you're proud of your own work. When you're a leader, you're proud of your team's work! Both are different levels of a business owner's personal evolution and journey!"*
>
> — AVADHI DHRUV

CREATING HARMONY WHILE MANAGING YOUR TEAM

A lot of business owners get trapped in analysis paralysis when it comes to making decisions in business, especially regarding managing their team.

One of my clients, Tim, was feeling overwhelmed because he was spread thin with having to manage his team's hours and workload, answering questions, checking whether everything was done yet or not, making sure nobody was slacking off, and deciding to check in on any employees' progress or wait miserably because he didn't want to hurt their feelings. Tim was afraid to lose the team member because he felt it would be hard to find another one, so then he didn't hold them accountable for the work to be done in a timely manner. That cost the business in terms of lost sales and other issues, and as you can imagine, Tim was in a complete downward spiral. This is all very common for business owners when trying to run a business. If you're feeling this way, like Tim was feeling, you're not alone. In this section, I will cover the three important aspects you need to have in place to be able to come out of the overwhelm, indecision, analysis paralysis, and actually be free and excited to grow your business further while enjoying your life!

To turn the situation around, I said to Tim, "The key to remember is that harmony has money in it! When there is discord between you, as the leader, and your team of employees and contractors, it can lead to dis-harmony, which is costly to your business and to your own mental and physical health."

The first thing for you to understand is that in order for you to create harmony in your company, your company's and brand's core values need to be very clear, as those core values are the basis that you and your team should always be operating from. When you have outlined a crystal-clear code of conduct, it guides your behavior and the behavior of your team, even in your absence. In fact, you must take the core values into account when interviewing for a new team member and ensure that this new person is a good match with the core values and wants to be on your team because of those!

Your overall mission and a long-term vision are also key components that differentiate your brand from any other, and also guide your team in terms of what to focus on from a big picture perspective, while they stay connected to the everyday tasks and projects they're doing.

Then you need to create your key intentions and top goals for the current year, which then need to be broken down into quarterly rocks. Having clarity on what to exactly focus on during each quarter is absolutely key for you and your team to be consistently on the same page, and then they can really function without you micromanaging every single piece of the business operations. This way they can get things done without needing your constant attention!

After understanding and implementing all of the above, Tim now lives in a completely new reality! He has the freedom to rest and enjoy his life (which is basically the entire reason why he wanted to have a business in the first place) while his team executes all aspects of his business with high standards and quality precision. This is the best feeling in the world for him! He can now relax, because the guidelines, such as the code of conduct, big picture clarity, and the detailed goals with quarterly focused rocks, are doing the job of guiding his team and keeping his business on track, while he has fun and focuses his time on celebrating the *wins* with his family and his team. (No more micromanagement needed)!

The three elements described above help to create harmony, and as I mentioned previously, harmony has money in it. When you are in harmony with your team, and the team is operating in harmony with the business objectives and goals, the business automatically starts to grow and becomes more profitable. People within the business, and the ones who are interacting with the business, all become happier and more fulfilled when there is harmony, and this naturally creates more money to come in and stay in, attracting abundance toward you!

In this chapter, you have learned the transformative power of delegation and synergy between personal and professional responsibility dynamics, illustrating how nurturing both your passion and family businesses concurrently can lead to sustainable success. By building a brand-aligned team, and fostering familial harmony within the business environment, you pave the way for a legacy of prosperity and fulfillment for generations to come.

8

PUTTING THE PAST IN THE PAST

As you embark on a new journey ahead, filled with untold possibilities and exciting opportunities, it is essential to take a moment to acknowledge and congratulate yourself for reaching this point in your life.

Your presence in taking the time to read this book signifies your commitment to embodying your highest spirit. So, take a deep breath and allow this moment to sink into the depths of your heart, and feel the congratulatory vibes from my heart to yours.

Today, as you read this chapter, the focus revolves around initiating this new endeavor for you with elevated spirits, taking the first steps toward a journey of growth. I'll delve into a few key points to guide you through this process below.

TURNING PROCRASTINATION INTO PROGRESS AND GROWTH

Sara found herself procrastinating on an important project she needed to complete, and she was afraid of the deadline coming up soon. So she started to get worried about what would happen if she didn't finish this project in time. She came to me and asked me how to get out of the procrastination she was feeling, and actually make progress on her project!

I told her this story of Jim who was also dealing with the constant procrastination in his business, and how he found the two bridges that made all the difference for him! So, Sara was curious about what the two bridges were about and how she could find them too.

Before you can find the two bridges, you need to understand the two worlds – the world of suffering and the world of joy.

Being in the world of suffering is caused by staying in resistance – resisting what is. This is where you're constantly in fear and worry. You're fighting circumstances and situations. You feel like a victim and feel that life keeps happening *to* you. You're trying to get things done in spite of all the troubles you face, and you're forcing an outcome out of yourself or from others. There is a lot of misery in this state.

The world of suffering is the downward spiral that causes your life to disintegrate. This is where you lose money, miss out on opportunities, have toxic relationships, and feel that your happiness is destroyed. This is where you are trying to swim against the current and it feels like a lot of effort and not much fun. This is where procrastination and struggle exist.

Fortunately, you do not have to stay in the world of suffering if you do not want to. There is a bridge you can take to get from the world of suffering over to neutral ground. This is the bridge of acceptance! By releasing and letting go of resistance and choosing acceptance instead, you can cross the bridge of acceptance and land on the neutral ground.

Now, neutral ground can feel much better than being in the world of suffering, but it is not a place to stay for long, because in this dynamic world if you stay here too long, you'll fall back into the downward spiral again. So, you need to take the next bridge to get over to the world of joy!

The world of joy is where you're in an upward spiral. More money and opportunities come to you naturally. You are in gratitude and celebrating your life.

So how do you get from neutral ground to the world of joy? By the bridge of surrender, of course!

The world of joy is where you allow the Universe to guide you. You trust the process as it unfolds. You have faith that everything that's happening in life is happening *for* you. It is for your highest good! You are able to give yourself grace, and love while being patient. You produce your best work and the highest quality results in this state. This is where progress happens effortlessly and turns into your business growth.

So, this is how you turn procrastination into progress and business growth.

First, recognize whether you are currently in the world of suffering or the world of joy. Procrastination mainly lives in the world of suffering, so if you're finding yourself procrastinating then you might most likely be in the world of suffering.

If this is the case, notice that. Then notice any and all resistances you may be experiencing, and then decide to take the bridge of acceptance. As you walk across the bridge of acceptance, notice yourself letting go of all resistances and allow peace to come into your field.

Now, you have reached the neutral ground.

Next, from the neutral ground, you notice that there is another beautiful bridge that you can now take, which will take you over to the world of joy! This is the bridge of surrender. Walk across the bridge of surrender and allow yourself to be taken by the Divine. Let yourself be carried, relax and embrace the loving support, release any fear and all the need to control, and experience what it feels like to flow with the current of life. Be in oneness with the Divine! You're now in the world of joy, and this is where all progress and business growth lies.

Stay in this state for as long as you can, and practice taking the bridge of surrender every day, to continue to produce your best work and highest quality results from being in the world of joy.

Make your work enjoyable for yourself. Make any important business decisions from being in the world of joy. If you ever find yourself in the world of suffering, first acknowledge it, choose to take the bridge of acceptance to get to neutral ground, and then slowly take the bridge of surrender to get to the world of joy!

This is how you turn procrastination into progress and business growth!

USING FORGIVENESS TO GROW YOUR BUSINESS

Here are five ways you can leverage forgiveness to grow your business.

First, when you set goals in your business, you are bound to achieve some and not hit the rest. When you achieve a goal, take the moment to recognize it and celebrate with gratitude. This is very important, most people get busy with their next goals and never take the moment to celebrate what they have actually accomplished. When you do not hit a goal, the emotional energy behind that can often get stuck in your psyche, becoming a subconscious block, and prevent you from moving forward. Use forgiveness as a tool in this case to propel you forward. Relieve yourself from the expectations you had set, release yourself from any disappointment you may have felt, and know that when you do your best, your best is good enough.

> *"Strength of character is the ability to turn bad luck into good luck, and that's alchemy. The ability to do this is in our power and control."*
>
> — AVADHI DHRUV

Second, when you are marketing your business and connecting with people, some people will like you, some people will love you, and some people will not even care. Some people may dislike you or seem distant and disinterested. When you get these various types of reactions from people, it can affect your sense of self and you can end up feeling judgmental toward yourself. This can become a subconscious block and a limiting pattern for yourself. Use forgiveness as a tool in this case to propel you forward. See yourself as a neutral person and the judgment others project toward you as merely a reflection of their own state of mind. Gift yourself the freedom to be you and share yourself uniquely with the people who are open and willing to hear what you are here to share. Know that when you are being authentic, the people who resonate with you are the people you need to surround yourself with and it is okay to let go of the rest.

Third, when you are having a conversation with someone who is interested in your product or service, this person may be a prospective customer or client, and when you offer them your time and attention, what you are doing is called sales activity. Your offering may be received and wanted by the prospect, or not. When you offer a product or service, and the prospect chooses to receive it in exchange for their energy or money, take a moment to fully receive and acknowledge the person, and make the exchange beautiful! If the prospect chooses not to receive your offering, it can feel like rejection. These feelings can get recorded in your subconscious mind as lack of safety and create self-sabotaging patterns. Use forgiveness as a tool in this case to propel you forward. Forgive yourself and remember that you are a child of God, a drop of the Divine ocean, a unique expression of the vast Universe. The feeling of being let down is a temporary part of this human journey, and an opportunity to learn a lesson about something specific and then move on. Take the wisdom from that experience and let go of the remaining energy, so you can dust yourself off and take steps toward your next destination.

Fourth, if you have a business partner, and you have

certain expectations of each other's role in the day-to-day operations, when those expectations aren't being met, it can create a lot of friction and chaos in the business. Your subconscious mind may have some limiting programs that could be contributing to this relationship, so you will need to become aware of that and shift it. Use forgiveness as a tool in this case to propel you forward. First, seek to understand the other person's perspective, even if and especially if you don't agree with it. Let that person have the space to hold onto their opinions without casting any judgment toward them or blaming their behavior for the impact on the business. Next, realize for yourself, what you truly want and what your own boundaries are, and communicate those with clarity to the other person, a.k.a. your business partner. When you communicate what was missed or miscommunicated previously, you can be freed up and feel satisfied within yourself, and then the other person can also decide with clarity which way they would like to move forward.

Finally, when you have an employee or contractor as a team member supporting you in your business, and your instructions or directions don't land well sometimes, you may feel frustrated and confused about how to tackle this situation. Subconsciously, it may feel unsafe to trust in another person and you may feel let down which can affect your motivation. Use forgiveness as a tool in this case to propel you forward. Forgive the situation before you sort out the issue with the person. Understand that it is always best to attack the process and engage the people in the business. Whether you need to set clear boundaries, create new systems or processes, or improve communication, forgiveness allows you to create a safe space for yourself and your team members to start contributing toward a new and improved way of operating. Know that you are the leader in your business, and the example you set with your behavior and demonstration of your core values is what your team will watch and learn from. Be wise and be kind.

These are the five ways to practice forgiveness often and watch your business soar to new heights!

HOW TO START NEW ENDEAVORS IN THE HIGHEST SPIRIT

Every new beginning should commence with gratitude. Reflecting on the past allows us to recognize and appreciate the gifts it bestowed upon us. Take a moment to identify at least three things you're grateful for from your journey so far. Whether it's personal achievements, memorable experiences, or moments of growth, acknowledge them with sincerity. In my case, the biggest blessings I am grateful for are my parents and my team who have guided and supported me tremendously in the creation and release of my first book, *Inner Genius Outer Guru*.

While gratitude uplifts our spirits, it's also important to confront any lingering incompletions from the past. These low vibrational energies, if left unaddressed, can infiltrate your present and future, casting shadows of doubt and resignation over your aspirations. Acknowledging these incompletions will allow you to release their hold on you, freeing up space for new beginnings. I encourage you to release any burdensome incompletions that weigh on your energy.

Next, I encourage you to set clear intentions for your journey ahead. Setting clear intentions infuses your journey with purpose and openness to Divine guidance.

Intentions allow you to remain receptive to the unfolding of your life's journey, trusting in the wisdom of the Universe to manifest your desires in the most fitting manner. For instance, my intention for this year has been to conceive, nurture, and publish my second book, this one that you are reading! While the specifics remained uncertain before I began writing, I trusted in the process, embracing each step with gratitude and openness. Intentions are not bound by rigid expectations but thrive in the fertile soil of possibility, nurtured by our faith and receptivity.

To anchor your intentions firmly into your energetic space, I often facilitate Clear Intention Healing™ sessions with my clients. This guided process empowers you to release lingering energies of survival mode, rush, and scarcity, paving the way for your intentions to take root and flourish. To experience Clear Intention Healing™ for yourself in a private session with me, email my team at team@avadhi.guru.

Once you have cleared any low vibrational energy and set clear intentions, it is time to return to gratitude, acknowledging the seeds of intention you've planted with care. It is important for you to continue to nurture them with faith and unwavering commitment. Embrace your transformative journey ahead with gratitude, knowing that each step forward brings you closer to your highest potential.

> *"You can define your worth, and set yourself free from the past, so that you can create a new sense of direction for yourself with a fresh perspective and true wisdom gained from the past experiences."*
>
> — AVADHI DHRUV

In this chapter, you have learned how to use the bridge of acceptance and the bridge of surrender to go from the world of suffering to neutral ground and then from there to the world of joy, turning procrastination into progress and business growth. By practicing forgiveness, you can cultivate a mindset of abundance and create a foundation for growth and success ahead. Finally, you have also learned about the transformative power of starting new endeavors with gratitude, releasing low vibrational energy, and setting intentions with openness and willingness to receive without attachment.

9

FINDING AND OWNING YOURSELF IN THE WHIRLWIND OF THE FAMILY DYNAMICS

When you feel constantly bombarded by expectations from family members, it is easy to feel lost or like you're being pulled in a current and can't think for yourself. In fact, even after you meet all of the said expectations, you may feel empty within.

HEARING YOUR INNER VOICE

It is key to heed your own voice to create a healthy personal sense of accomplishment for yourself. You will need to let go of any attachments to other people's validation and approval. Thoughts like *What will he or she think if I make this particular decision or choose this particular route?* can plague you. Recognizing these thoughts and noticing them before making any decisions is absolutely critical to your success and fulfillment. Always check in with your highest self first before you fall into the trap of complying to other people's demands. Give yourself the time and space to commune with your innate intelligence and feel into what's right for you and what's not. As they say, what anyone else will think is none of your business.

What you will think about yourself a year from now, a decade from now, and a lifetime from now is the most important question you should ask of yourself. "Will I be proud of myself?" "Will I be a great example to my loved ones and future generations?" "Will I have learned something new and gained wisdom for myself through this experience?" If the answers to those questions are "yes" then and only then you'd be on the right track to move forward. Always evaluate wisely before committing to anything. Take your time and do not let anyone or anything rush you. You deserve to have your own reflection of all your choices and then make the final decision. This is not to say that you don't make quick decisions, in fact, with Divine guidance you can make very quick and on point decisions with high levels of awareness, and money loves fast action so you will be rewarded very handsomely for being in tune with your inner genius and using that power to make important decisions. However, don't let anyone outside of your innate intelligence call the shots for you. Remember, you always have free will, and can choose to live your life exactly how you want to, do what you desire, and be who you wish to be. What you do with your free will is none of anyone else's business.

> *"Having a sense of worthiness, from within, is what will create the confidence that you are seeking to be able to achieve your goals."*

— AVADHI DHRUV

Let go of the need to explain and justify any of your decisions. When you own your desires and trust that your path is being illuminated by an all-knowing intelligence, you are always on the right path and can never be off track. You can lead by example and trust the process. Nobody else needs to understand where you're coming from, and while you can communicate with them and inform them if that's necessary, you don't need to wait for anyone's permission to move forward in the direction of your destiny.

When you learn to respect yourself, you will also need to set standards for others to meet you at. People will treat you as you treat yourself. So, if you don't value your time and energy, if you don't command respect and honor for your contributions, you'll attract the same kind of response from others. Our relationships are meant to be mirrors for us, so you may notice that the relationships in your life and business may be showing you who you are being, and if you would like to change anything that's showing up in the mirror, focus inward and change from within. Start knowing the value of your time and attention, and only give yourself to the causes that are worthy of you. Let go of any distractions and just rescind your energy by taking away your attention from people and situations that are not worthy of your life. You do not need to say yes to everything and everyone. In fact, it is only when you say no to certain low vibration elements that you create the sacred space for the beautiful high vibration elements to show up and shine in your life. Create space by focusing your attention on what's most important to you, by letting go of everything that isn't serving you and then let go of some more. Most of all, let go of the addiction to suffering that you may have been born into, and what isn't serving your highest good right now. Be transparent with your communication, and respect other people's free will. Leave them be and keep moving forward with grace and ease.

> *"The 'Survival Mode' is a result of not knowing who we truly are. The 'Creation Mode' is about knowing, experiencing, and expressing who we truly are!"*
>
> — AVADHI DHRUV

Owning your sense of worth, individuality, self-expression, and confidence is key for both your business success and family harmony.

CONFIDENTLY MAKE DECISIONS

Facing decision fatigue, living in constant dilemmas, and procrastinating on making key decisions in business and in life are common things that may be plaguing your day-to-day. You may find yourself flip-flopping between this way to go versus that way to go and not being able to make a clear choice and stick with it. If this has been a struggle for you, if you feel like you may make the wrong decision and regret it, or if you're afraid to make a mistake through your decisions, this section of the book is for you. I have dealt with dilemmas and decision fatigue myself and have helped my clients with this on a very intimate level. Making big decisions in business and life can be scary, and require a lot of internal clarity, so here are some things to keep in mind when you need to make a decision that you don't want to mess up!

First of all, see yourself as fully capable of making the

best decision for yourself. You know exactly what's right for you in your heart, so you don't need anyone else to tell you what to do! Tune out all the external noise and tune in within, this is very important!

Now, hold the intention in your mind that you always stand for what is in the highest good for all people involved. You make decisions from the abundance mindset, so there is a possibility in that paradigm for a win-win for all! When you're clear on your intention of a *win* for all and connect with that possibility, then the best options for a great solution can come through to you.

Scarcity mindset can keep you feeling limited in what's possible, so if you're in that mode, you should notice that by just becoming present to how you feel and then shift that constraining feeling to become more expansive first. Only after you have expanded your awareness and the state of being to one of joy and abundance, then look at all the options that seem available to you – and know that other options are possible as well which you may not even know exist. Be open to all the possibilities!

Focus on the facts and remove the layer of emotions that may be clouding your judgment.

At the end of the day, remember that no matter what you choose, you are always on your Divine path. I used to wonder if I was on my path or not, but the thing is, I realized that there is only one path. There is no way to be "off track" because there is only one track and that's the one you're already on! Now, you may choose to have different experiences while being on the same track. You may choose to be miserable, or you may choose to be content, you may complain and blame or you may trust the process, you may doubt and self-sabotage your actions or you may believe in your capabilities and own your power which comes from making decisions and taking actions – it is all up to you. Life is a game, and how you choose to live it is all up to you! My wish for you is that you choose to live it gracefully and thrive. Give yourself the freedom of choosing your own experience of joy, and then share the happiness with the world.

THE ULTIMATE TRUTH OF THE DIVINE PATH

Life is full of unexpected twists and turns. It is, therefore, important to stay grounded in your truth and your values. Knowing who you are, at your core, is essentially all you need to be able to navigate the path ahead and stay true to yourself through your embodiment. Always remember that your actions speak louder than your words. Be firmly rooted in your character, be kind with your words, and be clear in your actions. Communicate with your intentions and speak your truth without hesitation. Allow the Divine to guide you in your journey as you step into your fullest, brightest, biggest self. This life is no less than an adventure. Be raw and real when you need to be. Don't bow down to anything less than what you absolutely desire and deserve. Stay tall and strong. Be considerate without losing yourself in the act. Be yourself first and know that other people are fully capable. They are just as capable as you are and can figure out their life just as you can. Nobody needs you to save them, and you don't need to be saved either. You're a victor, never a victim. The same applies to the others. See them as victors as well. See them flourish in their own ways, and watch life guide them to their own destiny as it is guiding you to yours. Sometimes paths cross and then they go their own ways.

It's just the nature of the paths. In fact, this is the ultimate truth of the Divine Path.

In this chapter, you have learned the importance of finding and owning yourself amidst the whirlwind of family business dynamics, the significance of hearing your inner voice, confidently making decisions, and staying grounded in your truth and values. By embracing your worth, individuality, and self-expression, you pave the way for both personal fulfillment and business success, ultimately navigating life's twists and turns with grace and authenticity.

10

ACTIVATE ATTUNEMENT: THE DIVINE UNION OF MASCULINE AND FEMININE ENERGIES

So far, in the journey through this book, you have learned various concepts, principles, techniques, strategies, and more. We have come a long way. You have understood how to tackle your inner world and how to respond effectively to your outer world. You now need to bring it all together into a higher realm of consciousness. Activating attunement is the final step in your strategic harmonization plan. In this chapter, we will explore what the Divine Union looks like, and how you can achieve it to create your desired results.

DIVINE UNION OF MASCULINE AND FEMININE ENERGIES

Masculine energy is about doing and feminine energy is about being. Masculine energy is also about providing, protecting, problem-solving, planning, and risk-management, logic and reason, while feminine energy is about caring, nurturing, trusting, being open and receptive, bringing in creativity and fun, being in touch with intuition, and going with the flow. When the two energies come together, they create the Divine Union.

Too much doing causes burnout. Only being leads to inaction and lack of co-creation in the physical reality. Striking the right balance between doing and being creates the ideal outcome, because now you are taking action to achieve your goals and being open and receptive to all possibilities beyond your individual control.

Let's understand this concept with the use of an example.

Chris was in charge of sales in his business and was under a lot of pressure. He needed to achieve the monthly revenue goal and for that he knew he had to make a certain number of calls each day to be able to reach his particular target. Doing this sales activity consistently requires him to be in his masculine energy of taking action.

Now, in order for him to be able to take consistent action and make those sales calls, he also needs a good night's rest, nutrition through food he eats, mindfulness, and recreation activities to keep his mind refreshed. It is important for him to be alert while he is having conversations with his prospective customers. He needs to be able to function at his optimal capacity, be present with the people he meets, and be receptive to any feedback he gets during the process. All of that requires him to also be in his feminine energy of being present and receptive in order to maintain a good balance.

So, when Chris is overly in his masculine and forgets to balance with his feminine energy, his performance quickly deteriorates. On the other hand, if he is overly in his feminine and forgets to step into his masculine energy, he does not do as much sales activity and this affects his business revenue goals.

As he learns to have a balance of doing and being, of giving and receiving, he can balance activity and rest, and achieve the best results.

TUNING INTO DIVINE GUIDANCE

Always remember that you have the ultimate business partner in God / Universe / Source. This is an abundant, loving intelligence that is always and forever, without a doubt, on your side. The Universe is also the ultimate provider and protector of all, and hence the fundamental representation of the Divine Masculine. In order to fully connect with it and receive its providing, you must tune into your Divine Feminine essence.

When you have such an amazing partner in business, you are never alone and can tune into its guidance, through your intuition, at every step as you move forward in your life. You can attune yourself to its rhythm and find yourself in the flow of this miraculous beautiful gift of life. Fall in love with it and rise in honor. Be appreciative of it as it is of you. See your own beauty through *its* eyes. As they say, beauty is in the eyes of the beholder, and who is a better beholder than the Divine?! Train yourself to view your Divinity through the lens of the cosmic Father and the loving bond that you already have with Him.

Stay in tune with this loving energy and you'll hear the symphony of life playing through your veins. You'll hear the music of this reality shower all the riches of the world over you. You'll see rainbows everywhere you go, and step in dew every turn you take. You will learn to embrace and surrender to its unconditional love, so you can leave behind the judgment and self-deprecation, replacing it with peace and harmony in all areas of your life. This is the true meaning of being alive.

> *"It is your responsibility to strive for your dreams and focus on your goals. The world doesn't owe it to you, but the Universe will support you fully when you courageously take the first steps."*
>
> — AVADHI DHRUV

EMBODYING DIVINE CONSCIOUSNESS

The best way to live life is to be with the loving intelligence of infinite abundance. It is the blissful consciousness that we call the highest self or God consciousness. This divine intelligence is collaborative and loves everyone and everything just as much as it loves you. Stay in that consciousness at all times and you will create win-win solutions, self-acceptance and self-reverence in your life and through your business always. This is what creates success. This is what brings you abundance because you embody success and walk as if you are worthy of it.

The Divine always honors your free will, and so you just need to give it your permission to bring you all the abundance and love that you desire. The divine feminine part of you knows that you are worthy, and it is open to receive with gratitude for life. God consciousness is the provider and the protector of all of life, including you. It is the only source of all creation, and the only love you ever need. It can use many different vehicles and channels to bring love, abundance, and all of your desires to you in this three-dimensional physical plane, so it is important to be open to receiving from all different channels and stay curious about all the different possibilities that exist in the quantum field. You never know where something could find you from, and with Infinite Intelligence, anything is possible. That's the divine masculine that provides everything and can never run out.

The key is to trust in the unknown, allow yourself to open up and receive, and expand your comfort zone to be bigger and bigger so you can contain what's being given to you. You need to practice receiving so you can digest it in a way that enriches your life now and for many generations to come. By embodying the perfect blend of the divine masculine and the divine feminine, you can be a natural leader and role model in your family as well as your business. People will look up to you with respect and honor for who you are and what you stand for in the world. People will admire you for the possibilities and the strength you bring to the table. People will want to do business with you no matter the other choices they have. They will seek you out almost out of nowhere, because that is how the Universe works – it works in mysterious ways. You will realize that you have become a magnet for miracles. They will follow you wherever you go. You will notice that money chases you and comes to you, waits for you and waits on you, when you become this wealth magnet and are open to receive. You will no longer be chasing wealth and success. That is the power of the divine feminine when it merges with the divine masculine and becomes whole. Be clear on your values and stand for them no matter the circumstance. This practice will serve you well in your life as it has in mine.

Let the universal floodgates open and shine your light bright. Be yourself and be Divine.

FOOTPRINTS IN THE SAND STORY

One of my absolute favorite stories of all time is "The Footprints in the Sand." It goes like this:

> One night I dreamed a dream. As I was walking along the beach with my Lord. Across the dark sky flashed scenes from my life. For each scene, I noticed two sets of footprints in the sand, one belonging to me and one to my Lord. After the last scene of my life flashed before me, I looked back at the footprints in the sand. I noticed that at many times along the path of my life, especially at the very lowest and saddest times, there was only one set of footprints.
>
> This really troubled me, so I asked the Lord about it. "Lord, you said once I decided to follow you, you'd walk with me all the way. But I noticed that during the saddest and most troublesome times of my life, there was only one set of footprints. I don't understand why, when I needed you the most, you would leave me."
>
> He whispered, "My precious child, I love you and will never leave you. Never, ever, during your trials and testings. When you saw only one set of footprints, it was then that I carried you."

It was then that I carried you. What a beautiful reminder and insight!

"When you experience confusion, tune out the differing viewpoints around you and listen to your innate guidance within. It's the true source for leading you on your true path."

— AVADHI DHRUV

In this chapter, you have learned the transformative power of activating attunement by embodying the union of masculine and feminine energies and aligning with divine guidance. By tuning into the loving intelligence of the Universe and embracing divine consciousness, you pave the way for abundance, fulfillment, and success in both business and life.

ARE YOU READY FOR UNPRECEDENTED BUSINESS SUCCESS WITH FAMILY UNITY AND HARMONY?

"FACE the fear and DO IT anyway! If you want to live the life of your dreams, this is the ONLY way."

— AVADHI DHRUV

Once you understand the basic principles outlined in this book, it is important to know how to make a comprehensive plan for yourself and then implement it by tailoring it to the unique circumstances in your family business. As they say, all the knowledge in the world is for naught if you fail to apply it! In order to create tangible results in your business, and life, you must create your own strategic harmonization plan based on the process laid out in this book, and then allow it to play out in the reality of your life.

The three key steps to creating your plan are as follows:

1. Identify the key relationship dynamics in your family business that are impacting the

company's financial reality right now. Focus on the top three to five key relationships even if there are more to consider that you can think of. The first priority is to clarify the verbal and non-verbal agreements within the key relationships because this will create the biggest impact in your business.

2. Identify the main areas where there is a lack of awareness or understanding about the finances in your business. What are all the income sources bringing in revenue right now? What are all the various types of expenses, and which ones are helping versus hurting the business right now? What is the top priority to focus on and shift in terms of the finances so you can start to create or increase profitability for your business? These are important factors to understand further and even bring some of your family members into, so that true team effort can create synergy, enhancing your business' bottom line.

3. Introspect on your own emotions and notice where you feel fear, anxiety, scarcity, doubt, and lack of hope. It is very important to know your inner world as clearly as your outer world, so that you can shift yourself from within and create your ideal future from the inside out. In order to impact your family's future and build a lasting legacy, you will need to take a very close look at your internal state and consciously create a new reality. Your intention has the power to bring about

the biggest of miracles, and you reading this book right now is definitely one of them, so congratulations! Keep going, and take the right actions to welcome more magic and miracles ahead!

FURTHER OBSTACLES YOU MAY FACE

At this point, the clients I work with privately are able to create a strategic harmonization plan for their family business based on all of the steps we've covered in the previous chapters. Even after you have your strategic harmonization plan, below are the common obstacles that may come up as you go on to implement your plan.

Fear of Rejection

The fear of rejection can come up when dealing with intense family dynamics and relationships. When you feel afraid to say what's on your mind because you risk hurting a loved one or being misunderstood and retaliated against by a close family member, this fear is completely understandable and worthy of acknowledgement.

At the same time, staying in that fear is not in service to you and your health, neither is it going to help your family or your business. The best way to face the fear of rejection is to face it, rather than letting it lurk around in the shadows. If you are afraid of what someone will say when you stand your ground, you just need to do your part and see what actually happens as a result. Perhaps there will be some backlash. If there is, you'll have tools like compassion, patience, and clear communication to tackle that with. If there isn't, you'll be relieved, and the problem will be solved! Either way, going head on in the face of this fear is crucial to finding out the truth, once and for all.

Fear of Loss

The fear of loss can be pretty intense as well. You may be afraid of losing money, or afraid of losing time. It can even feel like you're losing something or someone very near and dear to you, when in fact, you are just setting some new boundaries and ground rules.

The true nature of reality is that everything exists altogether, and you're connected to all of it all the time, so there's really nothing to lose or gain for that matter. Everything just is, and the way you experience anything is by focusing on it with your attention and will. So, whatever you're afraid of losing is just an illusion. Knowing this, you can choose to have what you need forever, by focusing on it and bringing that reality to you. In my work, we do this through Clear Intention Healing™ and other powerful subconscious reprogramming methods that I facilitate. You and I can work together to bring anything you desire, right to you, by the power of your intention and thought along with aligned actions!

Fear of Losing Relationships

The fear of losing relationships can be the most intense to deal with. Especially when your loved ones are involved. Here's a verse I remember since I was a very young child: "If you love something, set it free. If it comes back to you, it's yours. If it doesn't, it never was." I truly believe in this. I deeply feel that it is the truth. I practice this in my life at every step I can and need to. Where in your life are you holding onto something with the fear of losing it? Who are you holding onto, afraid you might lose them? Know that your heart has all the answers, and it will guide you on the right path always. If something or someone is right for you, you can never lose them. If they're not for you, holding on is not going to serve your highest good. Trust the Divine within you and choose to let go of the grip.

Find the courage within yourself to breathe in the abundance all around you, inhale the love that's your birthright, and let go of any and all attachments. Release attachment to the past stories, relationships or people in your life, things and situations that are ready to be released, and bring wholeness to your being by creating space for something new. Something new that is worthy of your time and energy, worthy of receiving your love and care. Embrace the new blessings that are ready to come your way, because they are waiting just around the corner for your permission. The night is always the darkest right before dawn. Keep moving forward, and look ahead to your bright future, while sending peace and love to all, with gratitude for all the lessons learned and wisdom gained.

Fear of Abandonment

The fear of abandonment can be very difficult to navigate. It can feel like you're left all alone and you have nowhere to go. You can feel isolated and lonely. This is a difficult state to be in, and journey through.

If you face this type of fear, know that the only true friend you ever have is the Divine's love. That is the ultimate truth, and there is beauty and goodness in this abundant Universe. When you have the Divine within you, and all around you, and you're made in the image of its love, you have all that you could ever need, and you are lovingly held in deep caring hands you can call home. You can always rely on this Source as your abode. You are safe within it. You can feel blessed, cherished, adored, and fulfilled within its embrace. You are whole and complete in that moment, and you do not need anyone or anything outside of your connection with the Divine to feel happy and loved again.

Fear of Missing the Mark

The fear of missing the mark as an entrepreneur and losing potential growth opportunities due to family dynamics and challenges can be quite devastating to face. If you remember how excited you were when you started your business and saw the huge growth potential, you had dreams of achieving something great, and when all those come crashing down and feel like they're unachievable now, it can kill your entrepreneurial spirit and motivation for striving toward greatness. If only the family dynamics worked out, you could have achieved all those milestones and been as successful as you had wished to be.

Well, the truth is that you can have all that and more, when you realize that it's never actually too late to learn important lessons from past experiences and then move on.

The abundance mindset says that there are infinite multiverses and opportunities ahead if you choose to open up your perspective to new ways of being and doing things. You are capable of all that you dreamed of, and more. You only need to close some open windows, choose some new chapters to begin, and start to dream again, newly. This time, your dreams will be inspiring visions instead of wishful thinking. They'll have purpose and passion propelling them forward, and a beautiful, aligned team supporting their momentum. A creative culture, which comes from a heart-centered, conscious and aware collection of minds, can make every possibility a reality. You just need to believe in it again and take action.

All of the fears are ultimately one and the same, they just show up in different ways in different circumstances. The way to face any fear is basically just through recognizing it and tuning into your connection with the loving Source of it all. The more you rest in the embrace of all that is, you will be at peace. If you feel like you need a guiding hand, and a trusted partner who can shine light on this for you, in a loving and authentic manner that feels right for you, I'm happy to be that caring companion on your journey. Reach out to me through the various ways listed on the Gift for Readers page at the back of this book or via email at team@avadhi.guru.

> *"Constant dissatisfaction and struggle is a function of fear. Inner peace is a function of self-love!"*
>
> — AVADHI DHRUV

FORMULA FOR INFINITE EXPANSION

Welcome to the journey of infinite expansion! If you're here, it means you're ready to break through barriers, challenge your beliefs, and step into a whole new level of life.

The formula for infinite expansion is a transformative

concept that has the power to revolutionize your approach to growth and fulfillment.

Right off the bat, here's a disclaimer: If you are not looking for expansion, if you're not looking for growth in your life, if you're happy where you are and you want to stay where you are, and you're content with that, then this is not for you. Because what we're about to talk about, the formula for infinite expansion, is going to challenge some of your beliefs, perceptions, and ways of being.

So, if you are looking to break through barriers, if you are ready to look at any limitations that may be holding you back and grow beyond those to create a whole new level of life for yourself and step into a whole new version of yourself, then what I'm about to dive into is going to be perfect for you!

Step 1: Get Busier

We live in a busy world, filled with distractions, options, and ambitions. If you're feeling overwhelmed by the busyness of life, consider this: if you are busy, get busier. This might sound counterintuitive, but let me explain.

In 2023, I found myself overwhelmed with clients and responsibilities, and I thought I had no time for my passion projects like writing my second book. At the same time, I felt in my gut that it was time for my new book to be born into the world. So, I made a bold move and decided to take on this project. Right after I declared it and made my commitment, I started realizing that by taking on the challenge of writing this book, I automatically was able to streamline my priorities and found more efficient ways of managing my time and energy. My life, my team, and I suddenly became more efficient. As a result, I not only wrote my book but also created space for new clients and personal growth! Sometimes, getting busier with purposeful activities can lead to greater efficiency, clarity, and fulfillment.

If you still aren't feeling comfortable with the idea of getting busier, schedule your abundance call with me and I can help you get clarity on how to uplevel your life and get busier without stress.

Step 2: Create Bigger Problems

When faced with challenges, most people's instinct is often to avoid them or wish that they would go away somehow. You may think that once your current problems are solved, you will have no more problems and that would be the ideal state. However, what if I told you that creating bigger problems could propel you to new heights?

The truth to understand here is that every stage of your life comes with its own set of problems, and solving them at each level leads to your growth and evolution which brings you to your next level of blessings *and* the next level of problems. Instead of avoiding problems, embrace them and actively seek out bigger challenges. By creating bigger problems than what you currently seem to have, you can consistently expand your capacity for growth and unlock new levels of success.

Step 3: Expand Your Desires

If you're not getting what you want, ask for bigger things. Many of us settle for less than we deserve because we fear failure or rejection. However, by expanding your desires and aiming higher, you open yourself up to new possibilities.

Identify your deepest desires and dare to dream bigger. Whether it's in your career, relationships, or personal development, challenge yourself to aim higher and see what unfolds!

Overcoming Fears and Doubts

Now, you might be wondering: how do you face the fears that come with your current challenges?

Acknowledging and embracing your fears is the first step toward overcoming them.

By creating space for your fears and allowing them to exist without judgment, you can gradually diminish their power over you. Remember, growth often requires expanding your comfort zone and confronting your fears head-on.

Embrace the Journey of Infinite Expansion

Infinite expansion is not just a concept; it's a way of life. By embracing the formula for infinite expansion, you can unlock your full potential and create a life of abundance, fulfillment, and joy.

So, to summarize, here is the gist.

If you are busy, get busier.

If you have problems, create bigger problems.

If you are not getting what you want, ask for bigger things and expand your desires. Perhaps you are aiming too low and wishing for a life too small!

Whatever your desire, the Universe has a potential in its *infinite* field for it.

The only question is: Are *you* truly ready to receive it?!

12

CREATE HARMONY IN THE WORLD THROUGH YOUR BUSINESS SUCCESS AND FAMILY VALUES

If you have arrived at this chapter in this book, you have made huge strides and come such a long way in this journey with me! I am proud of you for sticking through it and being committed to your success and the legacy of your family ahead. Below is a summary of how far you have come.

THE STEPS TO CREATING BUSINESS SUCCESS AND FAMILY HARMONY

First, you learned to understand the importance of determining clear goals for yourself to focus on and that the goals need to be based on your own desires, not other people's expectations.

Then, you discovered the ins and outs of business and family relationship dynamics so you can overcome any pitfalls from masculine and feminine energy imbalances which are causing resentment, fear, and disrespect among family members, as well as leading to micromanagement and procrastination in the business. This allows you to prepare for the next steps of cultivating and implementing the abundance mindset by creating synergy and win-win-win solutions for all people involved.

Next, you were introduced to the concept of healthy boundaries – what they are and why they can be helpful for you, and you learned how you can start setting clear boundaries in your role with other family members' roles in the business, and as a result make new space for achieving your goals with the help of your relationships by switching conflicts into cooperation and alignment.

Thereafter, you understood fully that the business and family harmony you desire is not a solo task, it actually requires the magic of a team's effort, so you became clear on the importance of effective delegation, right hiring and training processes for team members, and how continuing to maintain healthy boundaries can help with running your family business effectively.

Then, you understood how to uncover and release any subconscious blocks that may be limiting you, realizing the patterns and habits not serving you, and strengthening yourself from within emotionally while putting the past in the past.

After that, you understood why it is important to know yourself and your values rather than trying to overcompensate for other people's demands, how to own your sense of worth, individuality, self-expression, and confidence, and why this is key for both your business success and family harmony.

Finally, you learned how you can step into your Divine Self, embody your true essence, and become in tune with your higher self by making God your ultimate partner in business and family life.

HOW TO CONTINUOUSLY GROW AND EVOLVE TO HAVE UNLIMITED SUCCESS

The first thing to know is that your inner world creates your outer world, and your life is a reflection of who you are within. So you can have your life look like anything you want by becoming the version of you from within that would create that kind of a reflection. Focus on becoming the version of you who would naturally reflect the life you want to live, and you can definitely have unlimited success, in fact, there's no way you can fail there.

The second thing to understand is that *you* are at the center of all areas of your life. All areas of your life are connected, just like the threads of a spiderweb, so when one area of your life improves, it will naturally bring other areas up with it. When you are feeling confident, you will make wise decisions in all areas of your life. Your career or business will naturally grow, and your relationships will get better too. When you learn to express yourself fully, you will attract more love and feel fulfilled in your work and relationships, have better health, and even bring in more money through your business. When you learn to create healthy boundaries, you will naturally set boundaries in your work and also in your relationships!

The next step is to realize that your business, and life, can be viewed as a chain with multiple links in it where each link represents a sub-area of the whole. For example, in business, you have sub-areas like sales, marketing, operations, accounting and finance, leadership and vision, team, and more. Each of these sub-areas can be likened to a link in the chain representing your entire business. It is important to note that when someone puts pressure on the chain, it will always break at its weakest link. Therefore, the chain is only as strong as its weakest link, and if we want to strengthen the entire chain, it would be wise to find and focus on strengthening the weakest link first. Once that weakest link is strengthened, it no longer remains the weakest one in the chain, and now it would be wise to find the new weakest link in the chain and focus on strengthening that one next. One by one, by finding and strengthening the weakest links in the chain during every iteration, the entire chain can keep getting stronger and stronger. In this way, identifying the sub-area in your business which may be the weakest link right now, and focusing on improving that one would serve to strengthen the entire business as a result. Continuing this process works very well in strengthening your business over long periods of time. The same principle applies to your family and life overall. This practice is an effective way to continuously strengthen the chain a.k.a. sustainably improve your overall business, family, or any other area that is important to you in your life.

A lot of times it's scary to focus on the weakest link in the chain by yourself, so you may avoid it. Also, a lot of times you may think that there is a plateau in an area and your dreams in that area of life are not possible. You may think that you have to settle in that area. However, the truth is that there is always an unlimited potential for growth in all areas of your life, including your business and family! Settling for less than your desires is actually what creates a cap on that area of life, so now you can choose a different reality instead.

Living your ultimate life requires you to have clarity on your ultimate goal. So, what is your ultimate goal in life? My ultimate goal is to become the *best* version of myself. If you choose to make this your goal as well, you must focus on becoming the *best* version of you in each and every moment, and as a result, you can live the life of your dreams.

Always remember that you are your biggest asset, and investing in yourself will always give you the highest return, hands down. No other investment comes close. I've invested hundreds of thousands of dollars and hours of study into my own growth and my life is a result of that. I have results in my life and with clients to prove it. So, what are you doing to invest in yourself?

I have created business programs for entrepreneurs and business owners, my team offers consulting and agency services, and I provide personalized solutions combining strategy with energy healing, so no matter where you are at with your business and what you need next, there is an offering my team and I have for you. If you need help getting clarity on exactly what the weakest link is in your business, and what would benefit you the most right now, reach out to me by scheduling a time through my website from the link on my Gift for Readers page! Life is really too short to be wasted and time is of the essence.

Work hard on self-improvement, work smart everywhere else!

Introspect on this: What is the weakest link in your business right now? What investment are you ready to make to strengthen that link? How much time, money, focus, and attention are you able to give it right now? How much more attention does it need from you as you progress ahead?

> "Life is not about driving on straight roads. Life is about beautifully navigating through curvy roads, on the way toward success & fulfillment. Always drive with love for others and compassion for yourself!"
>
> — AVADHI DHRUV

RETURNING TO ONENESS

Below is a journal entry I once wrote for myself as a prayer. If you wish, you may use it for yourself as well.

> *I and my Higher Self are one. I and my Divine Self are one. My Higher Self loves me and loves all others as they are all one with the Divine Consciousness as well.*
>
> *When I love, I also forgive. When I forgive, I do it from love. When I forgive myself, I release the world out of my love, and embrace each and every reality as valid and true in that moment.*
>
> *When I see the true nature of reality, I also become aware that we are all just mere actors on this planet in 3D, doing our best as to our given roles in each moment. We are mere models on a stage of the Divine, playing out our parts in the play. The director of the movie is the one that is guiding the flow, and that director is ever-loving and kind. He is the Divine connector of all of it. He loves beyond limits, and in his reality there is no right or wrong, good or bad. He is beyond judgment and his only expression is compassion.*
>
> *When I become one with that Divine expression, I become at peace with myself and liberated for my soul to love freely. I come from a higher knowing that*

everyone is on their own journey and no one can impose anyone else's will on anyone else. Yet we can all influence and inspire a higher expression of the Divine from within us and then all around us.

I can stay connected to that joy and love from within, immerse myself in Divine service, and release any shreds of doubts over to the greater God. Trusting that the creator of the Universe has got this and moving in the flow of Its guidance is key to harmony. I can just check status, take inspired action when needed, and then let go.

Now, I will just see if an action is aligned with the Divine plan or if there is something I need to let go of, then take the appropriate action. I feel renewed and refreshed. <3

WHY I WROTE THIS BOOK

I wrote this book because it was brought to me by Source. In fact, I was divinely tricked into it from birth!

If I hadn't been born into a family that has generational business blood in it, if I hadn't been exposed to business concepts since childhood and throughout my life without even realizing it, if I hadn't been pulled into the family business dynamics due to my family's unity, peace, and harmony being at risk, I probably would never have been able to learn enough to be writing this book here today.

When I was little, I admired my dad as my role model. I was always so proud that my dad was a businessman. I thought that was the coolest thing in the world! He wore these nice suits with button-pressed shirts and ties that my mom helped pick out for him. He had nice briefcases he would take with him to the office and on business trips. He would travel internationally and bring me the best, most amazing clothes and toys from around the world when he returned back home.

After his customer meetings, we couldn't wait for him to come back home and open up his big bag full of chocolates and goodies. It was like a treasure trove of surprises especially for us kids (me and my brother)! I knew he would always bring my favorite games or the stamps collection album when I had taken up stamps collection as a hobby or coins album for coins collection as my new interest. He always said that my mom is his queen, and I am his princess! I always felt like a princess with him around. I loved seeing his happy face after the long flights and all of the hard work he did during his workdays and then when he came back home, feeling satisfied to be with us, his family. I saw my dad as a capable and proud provider, just as my grandfather had intended to raise him.

With my grandfather and my dad as my two masculine energy role models, I also had my mom as my feminine energy role model. When I saw my dad ask my mom for her design choice, as my mom decorated everything in our home and organized so meticulously every little detail of the cupboards and the rooms, I saw admiration in my dad's eyes for her. When she dressed up in a traditional saree, as I grew up in India, I saw my dad looking at her complimenting how beautiful she was, truly. I saw the stunning image of admiration in my mom and dad's eyes for each other. That is what I grew up wanting in my life. The way my mom made a particular recipe of Indian food was completely out of the world, she got compliments from everywhere for her curries even after my parents and I moved from India to the U.S. due to the business expansion.

Growing up in a joint family house with my grandparents, uncles, cousins, and parents all under one roof, I have seen the polarity of masculine and feminine energies, and the balance through the interplay of generational harmony in a happy, healthy, and prosperous environment. When the years passed by and I grew up and went to college in the United States, I was away from family and lost touch with the childhood memories while exploring the world of adulthood. After college, as I took a job in the corporate world here in the US, I was busy building my own career and trying to figure out my path ahead as an engineer and manager. I had no idea or plan to become closely involved within the family business that to me had just been a part of my childhood and an integral part of my family's happiness at its core.

As I started to hear from my mom that my dad had been stressed because of the business, and some of the conversations within the family had been stressful, my heart started to sink. I had always seen harmony and joy in my family that was contributed by the business and so the thought of the business causing strain in my family and relationships was very strange and taxing for me especially when I imagined my dear dad being unhappy and struggling with certain aspects in the business.

As I tried to find out more about what was going on, I found that the dad I had seen in my childhood who was so driven and ambitious about all the business activities had somehow turned into a man who was no longer motivated to strive for growth, because his main concern had become the legacy of the business and the confusion about its succession. In the family business, me being the only child to my parents and being the only daughter, I was confused whether I was supposed to be the successor who provides that peace of mind to my dad about the legacy of the business he had spent his entire life building. Or was I supposed to be the person to help him find a successor who could still carry forward the business into the future? In my confusion, all I could think of was the fact that my dad was stressed and unhappy and as a daughter who loves her father dearly, I could not sit around and not do anything or try to help. I started to have conversations with my dad to find out what was really troubling him further and go deeper into the discovery process. That one decision made from the heart changed everything for me.

Today, I strongly believe that family harmony and successful businesses are very important for our world. When family members come together for a unified purpose and create a thriving business through their collective strengths, they can bring unprecedented value in the marketplace and foster beautiful employment opportunities for team members. In my family business, we have cultivated the best company culture because of our innate family values. You can do the same from your own perspective and bring loving energy to the world through it. Families bring soulfulness to businesses, which is what our world needs more of. So, I wrote this book to encourage more families to create thriving businesses, and to guide existing family businesses to foster more harmony along with their success.

If you are reading this and have come so close to the end of this book, it tells me that there is the same kind of desire and passion in you that I found in me. Perhaps there is a daughter or a son inside of you too who wants to see your father or mother happy. Perhaps you are a parent who has dreams of leaving a legacy for your children and grandchildren, and possibly be an example of health, harmony, and prosperity for many of your next generations to come. No matter your cause and the overall intention, there is a way ahead for you and that is the Path to Divine Harmony. Revel in all that you have learned in this book and take steps to implement the wisdom. You will reap many rewards from doing this for yourself and your family business, so then you can be a part of creating Heaven on Earth through peace, love, happiness, and joyful abundance forever and ever into millennia ahead.

ACKNOWLEDGMENTS

Thank you, dear family, for the lessons you gave me which have turned so beautifully into this book!

Thank you, Source, for bringing my soul into this lifetime and giving me the gift of this perfect family that I get to love, learn from, cherish, and adore!

Thank you, my dear parents, for who you are and for all that you do for me. I am truly grateful for your immense support in the process of birthing this book into the world!

Thank you, Angela and The Author Incubator team, for bringing this beautiful gem of a book into existence with such ease and grace. I am beyond blessed and grateful to have you all!

Thank you, my dear team at Avadhi.guru™, for your heartfelt words of encouragement every step of the way as I was dealing with personal challenges while writing this book. You held the torch up high while I was walking on the path laid out before me. You have always been on my side, through thick and thin, and that I am forever grateful for!

Thank you, my dear husband, for encouraging and supporting my many creative pursuits, such as this book!

Thank you, dear reader, for your passion and commitment to yourself, your family, the community, and our world. It is your courage that makes this Planet Earth a peaceful place. You deserve to live your most abundant life, and remember that you get to make a difference for the world in the many generations to come ahead. I salute you for allowing your heart to lead and for your brain to follow. It is only with humans like you that we can create the Heaven on Earth that I dream of creating through my work here in this lifetime on Planet Earth!

ABOUT THE AUTHOR

Avadhi Dhruv is an international bestselling author, YouTuber, and a business guru. She helps leaders of family legacy businesses run their companies in a way that fosters healthy family relationships.

Avadhi founded the brand, Avadhi.guru™ with the intention of bringing a holistic approach to businesses. She finds fulfillment in helping entrepreneurs gain clarity and confidence in achieving their business dreams. Through her books and programs, Avadhi helps her clients create and execute on strategic plans for their businesses, where they have unlimited potential for growth in income, freedom in lifestyle, and a deep understanding of their worth as a business owner. Her first bestseller, *Inner Genius Outer Guru: A Heart-Centered Entrepreneur's Guide to Unlimited Potential for Growth in Income and Freedom in Lifestyle without Burnout*, was a huge success amongst entrepreneurs ready to create real income-generating businesses they love.

Today, Avadhi is a thought leader and world leader whose vision is to create a world of abundance and fulfillment by empowering heart-centered, conscious entrepreneurs to take their businesses to new heights. Her clients have included budding entrepreneurs to leaders of multi-million-dollar international businesses who have successfully made transformational changes in their businesses and lives.

Avadhi is the chief transformation officer at Prabhat, a global brand and family-owned business with more than fifty years of success. In a few short years, she helped the Prabhat group of companies achieve multi-levels of top-line and bottom-line growth along with the ability to thrive in any kind of economic climate. Avadhi uses her skills and experience coupled with powerful transformational tools to help her clients create long-lasting business results.

Avadhi was born in India and attended a residential school, a Gurukulam, which provided an environment of holistic education interwoven with spiritual practices. Upon moving to the United States, she attended Georgia Institute of Technology for her undergrad in Industrial and Systems Engineering. After graduating with honors, she moved to sunny San Diego, California, which is where she currently resides.

For more information about Avadhi, visit:
    https://www.avadhi.guru/about-avadhi.html

Subscribe to Avadhi's YouTube channel here:
    https://www.youtube.com/@AvadhiGuru

ABOUT DIFFERENCE PRESS

Difference Press is the publishing arm of The Author Incubator, an Inc. 500 award-winning company that helps business owners and executives grow their brand, establish thought leadership, and get customers, clients, and highly-paid speaking opportunities, through writing and publishing books.

While traditional publishers require that you already have a large following to guarantee they make money from sales to your existing list, our approach is focused on using a book to grow your following – even if you currently don't have a following. This is why we charge an up-front fee but never take a percentage of revenue you earn from your book.

☞ MORE THAN A COACH. MORE THAN A PUBLISHER. ✍

We work intimately and personally with each of our authors to develop a revenue-generating strategy for the book. By using a Lean Startup style methodology, we guarantee the book's success before we even start writing. We provide all the technical support authors need with editing, design, marketing, and publishing, the emotional support you would get from a book coach to help you manage anxiety and time constraints, and we serve as a strategic thought partner engineering the book for success.

The Author Incubator has helped almost 2,000 entrepreneurs write, publish, and promote their non-fiction books. Our authors have used their books to gain international media exposure, build a brand and marketing following, get lucrative speaking engagements, raise awareness of their product or service, and attract clients and customers.

☞ ARE YOU READY TO WRITE A BOOK? ✍

As a client, we will work with you to make sure your book gets done right and that it gets done quickly. The Author Incubator provides one-stop for strategic book consultation, author coaching to manage writer's block and anxiety, full-service professional editing, design, and self-publishing services, and book marketing and launch campaigns. We sell this as one package so our clients are not slowed down with contradictory advice. We have a 99 percent success rate with nearly all of our clients completing their books, publishing them, and reaching bestseller status upon launch.

☞ **APPLY NOW AND BE OUR NEXT SUCCESS STORY** ✍

To find out if there is a significant ROI for you to write a book, get on our calendar by completing an application at www.TheAuthorIncubator.com/apply.

OTHER BOOKS BY DIFFERENCE PRESS

Fundraising without Burnout: Radically Reimagining Philanthropy to Transform Your Impact by Radha Friedman

22 Millionaire Money Codes: Create a 7-Figure Legacy Business as a Real Estate Professional by Connie Grant

Always Bring Your Sunglasses: And Other Stories from a Life of Sensory and Social Invalidation by Becca Lory Hector

Living Intentionally after Loss: 8 Steps to Reclaiming Your Passion and Purpose by Maya Manseau

Breakthrough to Entrepreneurial Brilliance: Shatter the Invisible Barrier Holding Your Business Back by Alana Mills

The Empathetic Attorney: Advocating for Survivors of Sexual Violence through Trauma Informed Care by AnnaMarie Motis

Is This a Cult?: Confronting the Line between Transformation and Exploitation by Anne. L. Peterson

Founder to Exit: A CFO's Blueprint for Small Business Owners by Pam Prior

A Second Wind after Loss: A Guide to Health and Renewed Purpose for the Grieving Heart by Denise Sherman

GIFT FOR READERS

Thank you for reading!

I acknowledge you for giving yourself the time to absorb the wisdom shared in this book.

It is my wish that you achieve the highest level of success possible by speaking your truth and transforming your business legacy!

It is very important that you continue to move forward in your business pursuits after reading this book to apply the lessons in your life.

Looking for more wisdom and guidance in your business journey?

In order to support your business success further, I have created an exclusive playlist of video trainings specially for the readers of this book, where I walk you through powerful lessons and the immediate next steps you can take to solidify your profitable business that earns you your family's respect.

In this exclusive playlist called "How to Build a Cash Rich Business Series," you will learn about:

- Healing your relationship with money
- The energetics of money and how you can apply them to your business
- How to handle debt in a productive and uplifting way
- ... and SO *much more!*

Email team@avadhi.guru to get access to the exclusive playlist of video trainings I've created for you.

Also, if you haven't already, subscribe to my YouTube channel to receive regular insights on how to navigate the intricate dance of running a family business while maintaining strong relationships with your loved ones:
www.youtube.com/@AvadhiGuru

The business owners I work with have achieved the highest levels of profitability as well as harmony within their businesses and family relationships, and you deserve to have your personal and professional dreams come true also! If you are ready for your next level of success, schedule your Abundance Call with me at:
www.avadhi.guru/scheduling

Take your best next step and achieve the success that is in store for you!

OTHER BOOKS BY AVADHI

A Heart-Centered Entrepreneur's Guide to Unlimited Potential for Growth in Income and Freedom in Lifestyle without Burnout

INNER *Genius* OUTER *Guru*

Avadhi Dhruv

www.ingramcontent.com/pod-product-compliance
Lightning Source LLC
Chambersburg PA
CBHW072208070526
44585CB00015B/1250